Oxford AQA GCSE History (9-1)

Conflict and Ten

between East and West

1945-1972

Revision Guide

 RECAP   APPLY   REVIEW   SUCCEED

Tim Williams

SERIES EDITOR
Aaron Wilkes

OXFORD

OXFORD
UNIVERSITY PRESS

Great Clarendon Street, Oxford, OX2 6DP, United Kingdom

Oxford University Press is a department of the University of Oxford.

It furthers the University's objective of excellence in research, scholarship, and education by publishing worldwide. Oxford is a registered trade mark of Oxford University Press in the UK and in certain other countries.

British Library Cataloguing in Publication Data

Data available

978-0-19-843288-3

Digital edition 978-0-19-843289-0

10 9 8 7 6

Paper used in the production of this book is a natural, recyclable product made from wood grown in sustainable forests.

The manufacturing process conforms to the environmental regulations of the country of origin.

Printed in Great Britain by Bell and Bain Ltd. Glasgow

Acknowledgements

The publisher would like to thank Jon Cloake for his work on the Student Book on which this Revision Guide is based, and Ellen Longley for reviewing this Revision Guide.

The publishers would like to thank the following for permissions to use their photographs:

Cover: Ullstein bild/Getty

Artworks: QBS Learning

Photos: p17: British Cartoon Archive/Associated Newspapers Ltd./Solo Syndication; **p19:** Associated Newspapers Ltd./Solo Syndication/National Library of Wales; **p21:** The Granger Collection/Topfoto; **p23:** Punch; **p25:** The Granger Collection/ Topfoto; **p27:** The Herb Block Foundation; **p31:** The Advertising Archives; **p33:** British Cartoon Archive/Associated Newspapers Ltd./Solo Syndication; **p35:** Museum of Australian Democracy; **p41:** British Cartoon Archive/New Statesman; **p43:** Don Wright, 1961/Tribune Content Agency; **p47:** Richard B. Russell Library for Political Research and Studies/The University of Georgia Libraries; **p49:** Keystone-France/Getty; **p51:** The Herb Block Foundation; **p53:** Express Syndication Ltd; **p58:** Roy Justus Papers, Special Collections Research Center, Syracuse University Libraries; **p59:** Punch;

Although we have made every effort to trace and contact all copyright holders before publication this has not been possible in all cases. If notified, the publisher will rectify any errors or omissions at the earliest opportunity.

Links to third party websites are provided by Oxford in good faith and for information only. Oxford disclaims any responsibility for the materials contained in any third party website referenced in this work.

Contents

	RECAP	APPLY	REVIEW

Part one:
The origins of the Cold War

1 The end of the Second World War **12**

2 The Iron Curtain and the evolution of East-West rivalry **18**

3 The significance of events in Asia for superpower relations **26**

Part two:
The development of the Cold War

4 Military rivalries **32**

Contents

RECAP · APPLY · REVIEW

Part three:
Transformation of the Cold War

Introduction

The *Oxford AQA GCSE History* textbook series has been developed by an expert team led by Jon Cloake and Aaron Wilkes. This matching Revision Guide offers you step-by-step strategies to master your AQA Wider World Depth Study: Conflict and Tension exam skills, and the structured revision approach of **Recap, Apply and Review** to prepare you for exam success.

Use the Progress checklists on pages 3–4 to keep track of your revision, and use the traffic light feature on each page to monitor your confidence level on each topic. Other exam practice and revision features include Top revision tips on page 6, and the 'How to...' guides for each exam question type on pages 7–9.

RECAP Each chapter recaps key events and developments through easy-to-digest chunks and visual diagrams. **Key terms** appear in bold and red; they are defined in the glossary. indicates the relevant Oxford AQA History Student Book pages so you could easily re-read the textbook for further revision.

SUMMARY highlights the most important facts at the end of each chapter.

TIMELINE provides a short list of dates to help you remember key events.

APPLY Each revision activity is designed to help drill your understanding of facts, and then progress towards applying your knowledge to exam questions.

These targeted revision activities are written specifically for this guide, and will help you apply your knowledge towards the four exam questions in your AQA Conflict and Tension exam paper:

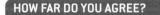

SOURCE ANALYSIS   **HOW FAR DO YOU AGREE?**   **WRITE AN ACCOUNT**

 Examiner Tip highlights key parts of an exam question, and gives you hints on how to avoid common mistakes in exams.

 Revision Skills provides different revision techniques. Research shows that using a variety of revision styles can help cement your revision.

 Review gives you helpful reminders about how to check your answers and how to revise further.

REVIEW Throughout each chapter, you can review and reflect on the work you have done, and find advice on how to further refresh your knowledge.

You can tick off the Review column of the progress checklist as you work through this Revision Guide. **Activity answers guidance** and the **Exam practice** sections with full sample student answers also help you to review your own work.

Getting your revision right

It is perfectly natural to feel anxious when exam time approaches. The best way to keep on top of the stress is to be organised!

3 months to go

Plan: create a realistic revision timetable, and stick to it!

Track your progress: use the Progress checklists (pages 3–4) to help you track your revision. It will help you stick to your revision plan.

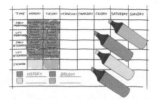

Be realistic: revise in regular, small chunks, of around 30 minutes. Reward yourself with 10 minute breaks – you will be amazed how much more you'll remember.

Positive thinking: motivate yourself by turning your negative thoughts to positive ones. Instead of asking *'why can't I remember this topic at all?'* ask yourself *'what different techniques can I try to improve my memory?'*

Organise: make sure you have everything you need – your revision books, coloured pens, index cards, sticky notes, paper, etc. Find a quiet place where you are comfortable. Divide your notes into sections that are easy to use.

Timeline: create a timeline with colour-coded sticky notes, to make sure you remember important dates relating to the three parts of the Conflict and Tension Wider World Depth Study (use the Timeline on page 11 as a starting point).

Practise: ask your teachers for practice questions or past papers.

Revision techniques

Using a variety of revision techniques can help you remember information, so try out different methods:

- Make **flashcards**, using both sides of the card to test yourself on key figures, dates, and definitions
- **Colour-code** your notebooks
- **Reread** your textbook or copy out your notes
- Create **mind-maps** for complicated topics
- Draw **pictures** and symbols that spring to mind
- Group study
- Find a **buddy** or group to revise with and test you

- Listen to revision **podcasts** or watch revision **clips**
- Work through the **revision activities** in this guide.

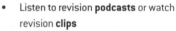

Revision tips to help you pass your Conflict and Tension exam

1 month to go

Key concepts: make sure you understand key concepts for this topic, such as conflict, tension, capitalism, communism, treaties, summits and alliances. If you're unsure, attend your school revision sessions and ask your teacher to go through the concept again.

Identify your weaknesses: which topics or question types are easier and which are more challenging for you? Schedule more time to revise the challenging topics or question types.

Make it stick: find memorable ways to remember chronology, using fun rhymes, or doodles, for example.

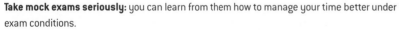

Take a break: do something completely different during breaks – listen to music, take a short walk, make a cup of tea, for example.

Check your answers: answer the exam questions in this guide, then check the Activity answers guidance at the end of the guide to practise applying your knowledge to exam questions.

Understand your mark schemes: review the Mark scheme (page 10) for each exam question, and make sure you understand how you will be marked.

Master your exam skills: study and remember the How to master your exam skills steps (pages 7–9) for each AQA question type – it will help you plan your answers quickly!

Time yourself: practise making plans and answering exam questions within the recommended time limits.

Take mock exams seriously: you can learn from them how to manage your time better under exam conditions.

Rest well: make sure your phone and laptop are put away at least an hour before bed. This will help you rest better.

On the big day

Sleep early: don't work through the night; get a good night's sleep.

Be prepared: make sure you know where and when the exam is, and leave plenty of time to get there.

Check: make sure you have all your equipment in advance, including spare pens!

Drink and eat healthily: avoid too much caffeine or junk food. Water is best – if you are 5% dehydrated, then your concentration drops 20%.

Stay focused: don't listen to people who might try to wind you up about what might come up in the exam – they don't know any more than you.

Good luck!

Master your exam skills

Get to grips with your Paper 1: Conflict and Tension between East and West 1945–1972 Wider World Depth Study

The Paper 1 exam lasts 2 hours, and you must answer 10 questions covering 2 topics. The first 6 questions (worth 40 marks) will cover your Period Study (Germany, Russia, America 1840–1895 or America 1920–1973). The last 4 questions will cover Conflict and Tension. Here you will find details about what to expect with the last 4 questions relating to Conflict and Tension between East and West 1945–1972, and advice on how to master your exam skills.

▼ **SOURCE A**

▼ **SOURCE B**

▼ **SOURCE C**

1   Study **Source A**. **Source A** supports/opposes... How do you know? Explain your answer using **Source A** and your contextual knowledge.

4 marks

2   Study **Sources B** and **C**. How useful are **Sources B** and **C** to a historian studying... ? Explain your answer using **Sources B** and **C** and your own knowledge.

12 marks

3   Write an account of how...

8 marks

4   '...'
How far do you agree with this statement? Explain your answer.

16 marks   SPaG 4 marks

REVISION SKILLS

Read the Period Study Revision Guide for help on the first 6 questions of Paper 1.

EXAMINER TIP

Don't forget to read the provenance (caption) for any sources you are given. It will give you valuable information and help you place the source in its historical context. You will be able to analyse what the source is saying (Question 1) and assess its value (usefulness) to the historian (Question 2).

EXAMINER TIP

Don't forget that you get up to 4 marks for spelling, punctuation and grammar (SPaG) on this question too.

REVIEW

Throughout this Revision Guide you will find activities that help you prepare for each type of question. They will help you recognise what a good answer looks like and how to develop your ideas to get a good level. Look out for the **REVISION SKILLS** tips too, to inspire you to find the revision strategies that work for you!

EXAMINER TIP

Don't forget you will also have to answer six questions relating to your Period Study in Paper 1. Ensure you leave enough time to complete both sections of Paper 1! You are advised to spend 50 minutes on your Period Study in the exam.

How to master source questions

Here are the steps to consider when answering the question that asks you how you know the opinion of a source.

Content

Look at the source carefully. You could label what you can see, or circle anything that you think is important. This might help you to break the source down and work out what it is about.

Provenance

Look at the date and other information in the source caption. The caption will give you a clue about what event(s)/issue/topic it is about. Think carefully about the events you have studied. Which one is the source about?

Context

Think back over your own knowledge. What features of the source content or provenance fit with what you know about the statement given in the question (such as 'Source D opposes or supports something')? What historical facts can you use to support your answer?

Comment

Make sure you use your own knowledge and information from the source to explain how the statement given in the question (such as 'Source D opposes or supports something') is shown.

 Spend about 5 minutes on this 4-mark question.

EXAMINER TIP

Try to describe at least one part of the source that either praises or criticises the event/person, then explain how this symbolises the statement in the question.

How to master 'how useful are the sources' questions

Remember that this question is similar to the source question in Paper 2, but this focuses on *two* sources.

Content

Look at and read both sources and underline or circle any detail that helps you to work out what they are about.

Provenance

Next, look at the provenance for each source; is there anything about the Time, Author, Purpose, Audience or Site (place it was created) (TAPAS!) that makes the source more or less useful?

Context

Now think back over your own knowledge. For each source, write about whether the content and caption fit with what you know. Does it give a fair reflection of the person, event or issue it describes?

Comment

You now need to make a judgement about how useful each source is. Try to use the sources together. What could a historian use them to find out about?

For each source, make sure you explain what is suggested by the content – and link this to your own knowledge to explain your ideas. You should also explain how the provenance makes the source useful (or not!).

 This question is worth 12 marks. Spend around 15 minutes on it.

EXAMINER TIP

Don't forget that every source is useful for something. Don't start telling the examiner what you can't use the sources for; no source will tell you everything, so just focus on what it *does* say.

How to master 'write an account' questions

Here are the steps to consider for answering the 'write an account' question. This question involves telling the key moments of an event in relation to the topic of the question. You need to describe, explain and analyse how one development led to another.

Select the key moments

What will you include in your story? Spend 1 minute to work out 3–4 key moments that are *relevant* to the question. Make sure you organise the moments in chronological order (starting with the earliest). You must include 1–2 specific historical facts for each key moment and plenty of specific historical detail.

Explain the connections

Write your answer based on the key moments you identified, and explain how the moments connect together to cause the event to develop. Make sure you link the story to the point of the question. A top level answer will also include an explanation of how the tension rises with each event.

 Spend around 10 minutes on this 8-mark question, but remember that this needs to include planning time.

EXAMINER TIP

Use phrases such as 'this led to…' and 'as a result of this…' to help you link back to the question and keep your ideas focused.

How to master 'how far do you agree' questions

Read the question carefully

What statement is the question asking you to consider? The statement is located within the quotation marks. Underline key words in the statement to help you focus your answer.

Plan your essay

You could plan your essay by listing other reasons that caused the event/issue:

Stated reason 1	Another reason 2	Another reason 3

Write in anything you could use as evidence for the different reasons, but remember that you only have about 2–3 minutes to plan and 15–17 minutes to write your paragraphs. For each reason, choose 2 historical facts you are most confident about and highlight these.

Context

Now that you have planned which reasons to discuss, start writing your answer, which needs to link to your knowledge as well. Aim for about 4–5 paragraphs: 1 or 2 that explain the reason named in the question and your own facts to back up the statement, 2 that explain 2 other reasons and facts to back them up, and a conclusion that explains your overall judgment.

Conclude

This question asks you 'how far…' you agree with the statement, so make sure you come to a clear conclusion.

Check your SPaG

Don't forget that you get up to 4 marks for your SPaG in this answer. It's a good idea to leave time to check your SPaG.

 This question is worth 16 marks. Spend around 20 minutes on it, but this needs to include time to plan and to check your SPaG.

EXAMINER TIP

Make sure you keep your ideas focused; use facts you know to support your ideas and use the wording from the question to make sure you explain how each reason led to the event.

EXAMINER TIP

If you want to achieve Level 4, you will have to reach an overall judgement. Is there one reason that you think is definitely more important than the others? Why?

AQA GCSE History mark schemes

Below are simplified versions of the AQA mark schemes, to help you understand the marking criteria for your **Paper 1: Conflict and Tension** exam.

Level	Source question 1
2	• Developed analysis of source based on content and/or provenance • Relevant facts and reasoning are shown 3–4 marks
1	• Simple analysis of source based on content and/or provenance • Some related facts are shown 1–2 marks

Level	Sources question 2
4	• Complex evaluation of the 2 sources • Argument about how useful the sources are is shown throughout the answer, supported by evidence from provenance and content, and relevant facts 10–12 marks
3	• Developed evaluation of the 2 sources • Argument is stated about how useful the sources are, supported by evidence from source content and/or provenance 7–9 marks
2	• Simple evaluation of 1 or 2 sources • Argument about how useful the source(s) are is shown, based on content and/or provenance 4–6 marks
1	• Basic analysis of 1 or 2 sources • Basic description of the source is shown 1–3 marks

Level	'Write an account' question
4	• A well-developed answer, clearly structured and explained • Explains different stages that led to the crisis • May explain how tension rises at each stage or how each stage linked/led to the next 7–8 marks
3	• A developed answer, well-structured and using a range of factual information to explain causes and/or consequences • Answer is supported by relevant facts/understanding 5–6 marks
2	• A simple, structured answer, using specific factual information to describe at least one cause or consequence 3–4 marks
1	• Identifies causes and/or consequences of the event 1–2 marks

Level	'How far do you agree' question
4	• Complex explanation of the reason named in the question and other reasons • Argument is shown throughout the structured answer, supported by a range of accurate, detailed and relevant facts 13–16 marks
3	• Developed explanation of the reason named in the question and other factors • Argument is shown throughout the structured answer, supported by a range of accurate and relevant facts 9–12 marks
2	• Simple explanation of one or more reasons • Argument is shown, supported by relevant facts 5–8 marks
1	• Basic explanation of one or more reasons • Some basic facts are shown 1–4 marks

You also achieve up to 4 marks for spelling, punctuation and grammar (SPaG) on the statement question:

Level	'How far do you agree' question SPaG marks
Excellent	• SPaG is accurate throughout the answer • Meaning is very clear • A *wide* range of key historical terms are used accurately 4 marks
Good	• SPaG shown with considerable accuracy • Meaning is generally clear • A range of key historical terms are used 2–3 marks
Satisfactory	• SPaG shown with some accuracy • SPaG allows historical understanding to be shown • Basic historical terms are used 1 mark

Conflict and Tension between East and West 1945–1972 Timeline

The colours represent different types of event as follows:

Blue: economic events   Red: political events   Green: military events

Black: international events or foreign policies

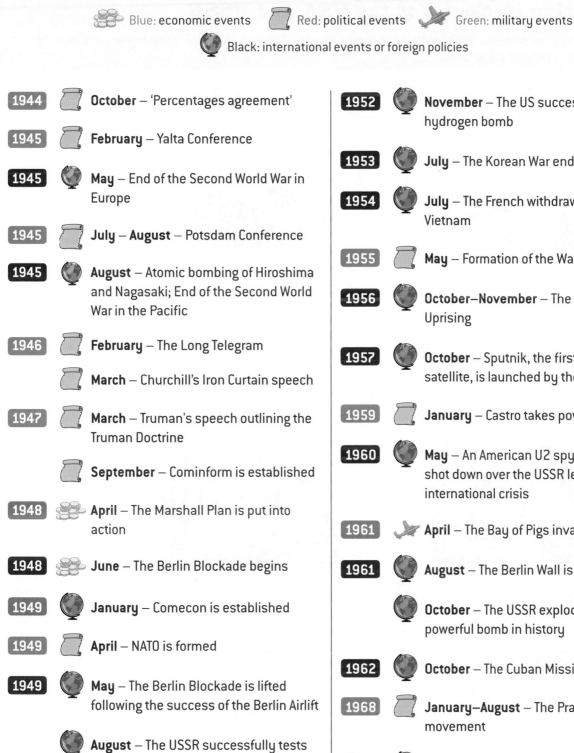

1944   **October** – 'Percentages agreement'

1945   **February** – Yalta Conference

1945   **May** – End of the Second World War in Europe

1945   **July – August** – Potsdam Conference

1945   **August** – Atomic bombing of Hiroshima and Nagasaki; End of the Second World War in the Pacific

1946   **February** – The Long Telegram

      March – Churchill's Iron Curtain speech

1947   **March** – Truman's speech outlining the Truman Doctrine

      September – Cominform is established

1948   **April** – The Marshall Plan is put into action

1948   **June** – The Berlin Blockade begins

1949   **January** – Comecon is established

1949   **April** – NATO is formed

1949   **May** – The Berlin Blockade is lifted following the success of the Berlin Airlift

      August – The USSR successfully tests an atomic bomb

1949   **October** – Mao declares the formation of the People's Republic of China

1950   **June** – North Korea invades the South leading to the Korean War

1952   **November** – The US successfully tests a hydrogen bomb

1953   **July** – The Korean War ends

1954   **July** – The French withdraw from Vietnam

1955   **May** – Formation of the Warsaw Pact

1956   **October–November** – The Hungarian Uprising

1957   **October** – Sputnik, the first man-made satellite, is launched by the USSR

1959   **January** – Castro takes power in Cuba

1960   **May** – An American U2 spy plane is shot down over the USSR leading to an international crisis

1961   **April** – The Bay of Pigs invasion attempt

1961   **August** – The Berlin Wall is constructed

      October – The USSR explodes the most powerful bomb in history

1962   **October** – The Cuban Missile Crisis

1968   **January–August** – The Prague Spring movement

1969   **July** – Neil Armstrong, an American, becomes the first man to set foot on the Moon

1972   **May** – SALT I

CHAPTER 1

The end of the Second World War

Contrasting ideologies of the USA and USSR

It is impossible to understand the Cold War without understanding the political and economic **ideologies** that divided the two superpowers – the USA and the USSR.

Key country: USA	Key country: USSR

• Developed out of the Industrial Revolution and the new social group of the middle class.	• Based on the ideas of Karl Marx in the nineteenth century and developed by Lenin in Russia.

• Private businesses and making profits are allowed.	• All businesses are owned by the state and all profits go to the state.

• Usually multiple political parties in elections. • Government usually elected by the people.	• One-party state, other parties are banned.

• Free economy.	• Economy controlled by the government.

• Great differences in wealth but most have a reasonable standard of living. • Based on the idea of 'opportunity for all'.	• Lower average standard of living, but wealth more equally shared. • Based on the ideas of fairness and equality.

Ideological differences

- The USA was a capitalist system and placed great emphasis on the 'American Dream' of individuals becoming successful and wealthy.
- The USSR was communist and its first leader, Vladimir Lenin, called for the overthrow of capitalism around the world.

Propaganda

- In the West, governments and the media spread fear about the communist threat to people's way of life. The '**Red Scare**' of the 1920s saw panic and arrests in the USA.
- In the USSR, Western governments were seen as a threat to the revolution and as the oppressors of workers worldwide.

The First World War

- Russia had fought on the side of the Allies until the revolution in 1917, when its new leaders withdrew from the war. Britain and France would find it hard to trust the Russians in the future.

The USA and the USSR: Why was there so much mistrust before the Second World War?

The Russian Civil War

- Following the Russian Revolution of 1917, the Reds (communists) and the Whites (anti-communists) fought in a brutal civil war for control of the country. Western countries sent troops to support the Whites.

The Nazi–Soviet Pact

- Despite their total opposition to each other's political systems, Nazi Germany and the USSR signed a non-aggression pact in 1939.
- In return for avoiding an invasion and securing territory in Poland, Stalin entered into an agreement with a government that had persecuted communists. The West saw this as further evidence that the USSR could not be trusted.

Stalin's regime

- Lenin's successor, Joseph Stalin, was brutal and ruthless in his rule of the country. The secretive nature of the regime along with the disappearance, arrest and murder of high-profile figures led many in the West to mistrust Stalin's government.

The Grand Alliance

- Despite the huge amount of mistrust, Hitler's invasion of the USSR in 1941 brought East and West together. The two sides united to fight their common enemy: Nazi Germany. By working together, East and West were able to defeat the Nazis in 1945.

 ## APPLY

HOW FAR DO YOU AGREE?

a Create a poster showing the main differences between capitalism and communism.

b Create a set of flashcards showing the main reasons for mistrust between East and West before 1945. Place your flashcards in order of importance, with the most important reason for mistrust at the top, and the least important at the bottom. Make sure you are able to justify your decisions.

c   'The main reason for distrust between East and West before 1945 was their ideological differences.' How far do you agree with this statement? Explain your answer.

EXAMINER TIP

Remember that the statement in the 'how far do you agree' question will only mention **one** reason or cause. You need to consider several in your answer. In this example, it mentions ideological differences but you should also include other reasons for distrust.

REVISION SKILLS

Making revision cards is a good way of revising and creating a useful revision aid for later use. Jot down three or four things under a heading on each card. Try to include a factual detail with each point.

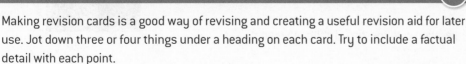

The Yalta Conference, February 1945

As the Second World War drew to a close and it became clear that Nazi Germany would be defeated, the Allies began to consider the post-war world.

The West's aims	The USSR's aims
• East-West co-operation should continue.	• East-West co-operation should continue.
• Germany should be rebuilt as an independent, democratic country.	• Spheres of influence should be created to guarantee security.
• Countries in Eastern Europe should have the right to **self-determination** and be free from outside influence.	• Germany should remain weak.
	• German industry should pay for the rebuilding of the USSR.
• The **United Nations** should be formed to help avoid conflicts.	• The World Bank and the IMF should have no authority over the USSR, but the USSR would be prepared to work within the United Nations (UN).
• There should be economic co-operation through the **World Bank** and the **International Monetary Fund** (IMF).	

Early discussions

- In December 1943, with the war still continuing, Stalin, Roosevelt and Churchill met in Tehran.
- In October 1944, Stalin and Churchill met in Moscow. Churchill wrote his idea about how to split Eastern Europe after the war on a table napkin, which Stalin ticked to show his approval. This became known as the '**percentages agreement**'.

The aims of Stalin, Churchill and Roosevelt

Winston Churchill

- Aware of Stalin's aims and wanted to protect British interests.
- Wanted a close relationship with the USA.
- Struggled to understand Stalin's point of view.
- As a strong anti-communist, he was naturally mistrustful of Stalin.

Franklin D. Roosevelt

- Committed to working with the USSR and got on well with Stalin.
- Believed that only a capitalist Europe could prevent a future war.
- Some argue that he misunderstood Stalin's aims and assumed they wanted the same thing.

Joseph Stalin

- Wanted to ensure that the total devastation suffered by the USSR during the war could never happen again.
- Believed that creating a sphere of influence around the USSR was the best way to ensure security.
- Recognised the need for co-operation with the West (although many of his ministers did not).

The division of Germany

Germany was to be divided into four zones – one each for the USSR, the USA, Britain and France. Berlin, which was within the Soviet zone, would also be divided in the same way.

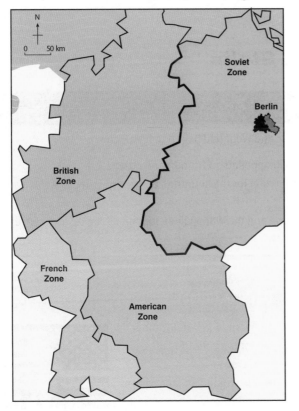

The liberated countries of Eastern Europe would be allowed to hold free elections.

The key agreements made at Yalta

The UN would be formed to ensure future co-operation.

'The Declaration of Liberated Europe' was signed, although there were differences in how this document was interpreted by the three leaders, particularly when it came to Poland.

APPLY

HOW FAR DO YOU AGREE?

a   Using the information on this page, copy and complete the Venn diagram showing the aims of the leaders going into the Yalta conference.

b   How far did the leaders have the same aims?

c   Who do you think would have been most pleased with the outcome of the conference?

d   **EXAM QUESTION** 'The USSR gained more of what it wanted from Yalta than the West.' How far do you agree with this statement? Explain your answer.

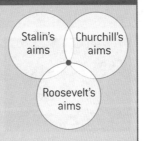
Stalin's aims   Churchill's aims   Roosevelt's aims

EXAMINER TIP

Make sure you leave enough time to write your essay in the exam. An essay answer should probably take you no more than 20 minutes.

The Potsdam Conference, July 1945

By the time of the next peace conference, in July 1945, Nazi Germany had been defeated and there had been a change in leadership for two of the Allies.

The aims of Attlee, Truman and Stalin

The Grand Alliance dissolves

By the time of the Potsdam Conference the unity between East and West had begun to break down.

- Stalin's desire to make Germany pay reparations was totally opposed by Truman and Attlee.
- Truman and Attlee wanted independence and self-determination for the countries of Eastern Europe. Stalin wanted them to remain under Soviet influence.
- With the USSR's **Red Army** occupying most of Eastern Europe and the war against Japan still raging on, the West simply had to accept the situation as it was.

Clement Attlee

- Focused on domestic plans, e.g. the creation of the welfare state.
- Worried about Soviet expansion.
- Wanted a secure Germany.
- Saw Britain as weaker and needing American friendship.

Harry S. Truman

- Wanted self-determination for the countries of Europe.
- Distrusted Stalin and his intentions.
- Thought America had the upper hand because of the atomic bomb.

Joseph Stalin

- Saw America as a rival and wanted security for USSR.
- Thought he was in a powerful position with the Red Army occupying Eastern Europe.
- Distrusted America now it had the atomic bomb.

Potsdam: the key agreements

- The division of Germany was confirmed.
- The Nazi Party was banned and its leaders put on trial.
- Germans living in Poland, Hungary and Czechoslovakia were to be returned to Germany.
- Poland was to lose some territory to the USSR.

The impact of the atomic bomb

- Truman's decision to drop atomic bombs on Hiroshima and Nagasaki in August 1945 ended the war in the Pacific.
- Although Stalin had been informed by his spies of the bomb's existence, Truman did not inform him officially. This added to tension and distrust.
- The surrender of Japan removed the need for Soviet troops in the Pacific and therefore the need for the Grand Alliance to continue.

SUMMARY

- Before the Second World War, the relationship between the USSR and the West was one of mistrust.

- The existence of a common enemy, in the form of Nazi Germany, brought the two sides together in a **Grand Alliance**.

- Tensions began to arise at the Yalta Conference, although some agreements were made, most notably on the issue of Germany.

- By the time of the Potsdam Conference, the Grand Alliance had disintegrated.

- The use of the atomic bomb on Japan ended the war and the Grand Alliance. It also drastically added to the growing tension and mistrust between the USSR and the West.

 APPLY

SOURCE ANALYSIS

▼ **SOURCE A** *Adapted from a description of the conference, written in 1945 by Walter Monckton, a member of the British delegation at Potsdam:*

> Truman would come prepared on each subject with a short, firm statement of US policy, and he kept repeating it. Stalin spoke quietly and in brief sentences. Stalin was often humorous, never offensive; direct and uncompromising. He had a trick of looking up when he was thinking or speaking, and much of the time he would be smoking a Russian cigarette.

▼ **SOURCE B** *A cartoon by the British cartoonist David Low, published in the* London Evening Standard, *30 October 1945.*

"WHY CAN'T WE WORK TOGETHER IN MUTUAL TRUST & CONFIDENCE?"

a Study **Source A**. What does it suggest about the relationship between Stalin and Truman at the Potsdam Conference?

b Now study **Source B**. Write a short description of the source in your own words.

c What point do you think **Source B** is making? Use details of the source and your own knowledge when answering.

d

> **EXAM QUESTION** Study **Sources A** and **B**. How useful are **Sources A** and **B** to a historian studying the reasons for increased tension between East and West in 1945? Explain your answer using **Sources A** and **B** and your contextual knowledge.

EXAMINER TIP

When looking at sources, it is important to consider when they were created. What had changed between the creation of these two sources?

WRITE AN ACCOUNT

a Make a list of the key areas of disagreement between the USSR and the West at the time of the Potsdam Conference.

b Now look at the agreements that were made. What problems remained?

c **EXAM QUESTION** Write an account of how the Potsdam Conference led to an increase in tension between East and West.

CHAPTER 2

The Iron Curtain and the evolution of East-West rivalry

 **RECAP**

Soviet expansion in Eastern Europe

At the end of the Second World War, the USSR effectively controlled most of Eastern Europe.

- The Red Army already occupied the land that they had taken from the Nazis, including Poland, Hungary and Yugoslavia.
- Communism was popular in Eastern Europe, after the horrors of Nazi occupation.
- The Soviets made it very difficult for non-communists to gain power in these countries by rigging elections and arresting and executing opponents.

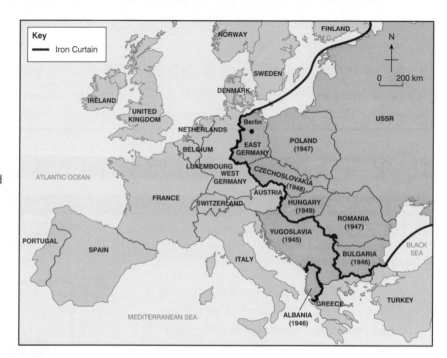

The Western response to Soviet expansion

1. The Long Telegram

As tensions grew, the US embassy in Moscow began to report back on developments within the USSR.

On 22 February 1946, George Kennan, the well-respected second in command at the embassy, sent a report back to the USA. It said that:

- he believed that the Soviets wanted to spread the USSR's influence as widely as possible
- the USSR saw the USA as its enemy
- any attempt at co-operation between the USA and the USSR would fail.

'The Long Telegram' (8000 words) confirmed President Truman's own fears and had a large influence on his future approach towards the USSR.

2. Churchill's Iron Curtain speech

On 6 March 1946, during a visit to the USA, Winston Churchill made a speech about the situation in Europe. As Britain's former prime minister and wartime leader, his views were to be taken seriously.

Churchill said:

- The USSR was attempting to spread its influence across the rest of Europe and increase its power.
- An invisible line had split Europe in two, between the East and the West. He called the line the **Iron Curtain**.

The term 'Iron Curtain' was widely used for the remainder of the Cold War. Truman, who was at Churchill's side when he made the speech, respected and shared Churchill's view. In Moscow, the speech was viewed as a deliberate misrepresentation of the USSR's aims.

⚙ APPLY

SOURCE ANALYSIS

▼ **SOURCE A** *A cartoon by Leslie Illingworth from the* Daily Mail, *6 March 1946.*

a Study **Source A**. What does it show? Describe what you see.

b **EXAM QUESTION** Study **Source A**. Source A is critical of the USSR. How do you know? Explain your answer using **Source A** and your contextual knowledge.

WRITE AN ACCOUNT

a Create a fact sheet to show the key features of the Long Telegram and Churchill's Iron Curtain speech.

b **EXAM QUESTION** Write an account of how relations between the USSR and the Western Allies changed between 1945 and 1946.

REVIEW

Look back at the previous chapter to remind yourself about the events of 1945. Turn to page 9 for further guidance on how to answer this type of question.

REVISION SKILLS

Having someone test you on your notes and revision is an excellent way of seeing how much you remember, understand, and still have to learn. Brief oral test sessions of about 10 minutes are best.

EXAMINER TIP

Remember to look at both the content of the source and its provenance (information about the source, such as who wrote it and when). You should refer to both in your answer.

EXAMINER TIP

For this question you will need to consider the relationship between the USSR and the Western Allies in the final year of the Second World War. This will allow you to make a comparison with their relationship in 1946.

The Truman Doctrine, 1947

The **Truman Doctrine** refers to the American policy towards communism after the Second World War. President Truman outlined the policy in a speech to Congress in March 1947.

Truman said:

- Communism posed a serious threat to the USA and the rest of the world.
- The USA would support any country that was under threat from communism.
- The focus must be on '**containing** communism' – keeping it within the countries where it was already established.

The purpose of Truman's speech was to make it clear to the USSR that its expansion into Europe had to end. It was also a response to the situation in Greece and Turkey, where it seemed likely that communism was about to take hold.

The Marshall Plan

While the Truman Doctrine established the USA's policy, it was the European Recovery Program that put it into practice. Known as the **Marshall Plan**, after the USA **Secretary of State**, George Marshall, it put billions of dollars into rebuilding Europe.

Purpose

The plan had three main aims:

- To aid economic recovery in Europe in order to stop people from turning to communism.
- To support the containment of communism within Eastern Europe.
- To create a market for American goods in order to build up the American economy.

The Plan

- $13.15 billion was divided among the countries that were willing to accept aid.
- Aid was offered to all the countries in Europe, east and west.
- Aid was supplied in the form of money or resources (e.g. machinery for farm work). All resources had to be bought from American suppliers.

▼ **A** *The amount of Marshall aid given to each country that accepted it*

Country	Amount of aid
UK	$3.2b
France	$2.7b
Italy	$1.5b
West Germany	$1.4b
Netherlands	$1.1b
Greece	$694m
Austria	$677m
Belgium/Luxembourg	$556m
Denmark	$271m
Norway	$254m
Turkey	$221m
Ireland	$146m
Sweden	$107m
Portugal	$50m
Trieste	$32m
Iceland	$29m

The results

- Marshall aid was vital for the recovery of Western Europe. It allowed economies to be rebuilt and the standard of living to rise.
- The American economy also benefited.
- It demonstrated that the USA was committed to involvement in Europe for the long term.
- Communism became less popular in Western Europe.
- The division of East and West became even more firmly established, as Stalin forbade counties behind the Iron Curtain from accepting aid.

 APPLY

SOURCE ANALYSIS

▼ **SOURCE A** *A cartoon called 'The Way Back' by the American artist D. R. Fitzpatrick, from 1947.*

▼ **SOURCE B** *Adapted from an interview in December 1995 with Vladimir Yerofeyev (1920–2011), a Soviet diplomat and Stalin's personal French language translator:*

> Stalin was suspicious and didn't like Marshall aid. He thought it was a ploy by Truman to allow America to infiltrate European countries. I think America never really wanted the Soviet Union and the countries of the Eastern bloc to benefit from Marshall aid. After all, they made no further effort to persuade them to take part.

a Create a mind-map of the Truman Doctrine and the Marshall Plan.

b Study **Source A**. What does it show? Describe what you can see.

c What opinion do you think the source puts forward about the Marshall Plan?

d Now look at **Source B**. What does it tell you?

e Do you think the writer sees the Marshall Plan in the same way as the creator of **Source A**? Why?

f Study **Sources A** and **B**. How useful are these to a historian studying the Marshall Plan? Explain your answer using **Sources A** and **B** and your contextual knowledge.

EXAMINER TIP

Remember to consider the provenance of the source, such as who wrote it and when, as well as its content. You should generally assume a source is useful, but think about how the source's origin might affect *how* it is useful.

Stalin's reaction: Cominform and Comecon

Stalin reacted negatively to American policies on communism and its activities in Europe after the Second World War.

Stalin's response to the Truman Doctrine: Cominform

- Stalin saw the Truman Doctrine as a direct threat to communism.
- He created the Communist Information Bureau (**Cominform**) to ensure unity in Eastern Europe.
- All Cominform member countries would meet regularly in Moscow to ensure that they were all following the same policies.

Stalin's response to the Marshall Plan: Comecon

- Stalin saw the Marshall Plan as an example of '**dollar imperialism**' by the USA. He thought that the USA gained power over countries that accepted their aid and was fearful that they were using this power for world domination.
- He made it clear that Eastern European countries should not accept any aid from the USA.
- In 1949, he created **Comecon**, a Soviet alternative to Marshall Aid. Countries who signed up to Comecon were agreeing to work together and share resources in what was officially a union of equal partners.
- In reality, all decisions were made in Moscow.

Yugoslavia: a problem for Stalin

Unlike other communist countries in Eastern Europe, Yugoslavia did not owe its freedom from the Nazis to the Red Army. Its leader, Tito, therefore had no particular loyalty to Stalin. Although their relationship was good at first, things began to go wrong:

- Tito was unwilling to follow all of Stalin's instructions. He saw Yugoslavia as an independent country.
- In 1948, Tito accepted Marshall aid, something that Stalin had specifically forbidden. Yugoslavia was the only communist country to accept this aid from the USA.
- From this point, Yugoslavia's position was unique: a communist country that was not behind the Iron Curtain.

 **APPLY**

HOW FAR DO YOU AGREE?

a Create a spider diagram showing Stalin's response to USA policies towards Europe between 1946 and 1949.

b In what ways did Stalin's responses lead to further division in Europe?

c Who do you think was most responsible for the division of Europe after the Second World War: the USA or the USSR? Explain your answer.

d EXAM QUESTION — 'The main reason for increased East–West rivalry between 1947 and 1949 was the Marshall Plan.' How far do you agree with this statement? Explain your answer.

> **EXAMINER TIP**
> This question requires you to consider other reasons for increased tension during this period, not just the Marshall Plan.

REVIEW

Remind yourself why the East and West were so divided by looking at pages 18–21.

SOURCE ANALYSIS

a Study **Source A**. What does this source show? Who do you think the people in the street are?

b What event is the source depicting?

SOURCE A *A cartoon from the British magazine* Punch *by EH Shepard, published in 1948. The figure opposite Stalin is the Yugoslav leader, Tito.*

c EXAM QUESTION — Study **Source A**. Source A is critical of the USSR. How do you know? Explain your answer using **Source A** and your contextual knowledge.

> **EXAMINER TIP**
> First, work out what the source shows. Labelling a couple of the key features might help you to do this in the exam. Then, link these images to what you know about the event: your contextual knowledge. Also consider when the source was produced. What was happening at that time?

The Berlin Blockade and Airlift, 1948–49

Causes

- The division of Berlin had been agreed at Yalta and Potsdam and had been in place since the end of the Second World War. Initially, the Allies worked together to run Berlin through the **Allied Control Council** (ACC). This became increasingly difficult as time went on.
- The Western Allies were keen for Germany to be rebuilt and unified, but Stalin opposed this as he saw Germany as a potential threat.
- In March 1948, the Western Allies agreed to unify their sectors of Germany and Berlin, and to introduce a new currency. Stalin did the same in the East.
- The USSR's ultimate aim was for the withdrawal of all Western officials from Berlin. From April 1948, the Soviets began to make life difficult for them.

The Blockade

- From April 1948, the '**mini-blockade**' began. It included blocking military supply routes, traffic restrictions and closing bridges for 'maintenance'.
- Tensions increased after a British and a Soviet plane collided on 5 April and violence broke out.
- On 24 June 1948, Stalin launched a full blockade. Transport links were blocked into West Berlin – no food, fuels or medical supplies could reach people in the non-Soviet part of the city. Electricity supplied from within the Soviet sector was cut.
- For the 2.5 million inhabitants of West Berlin, the situation quickly became very serious.

The Western Response

- Truman and Atlee were both determined not to give in.
- The West's first response was a counter-blockade that stopped trains travelling out of West Berlin. This had a limited impact.
- On 26 June 1948, British and American planes began delivering supplies to West Berlin. At its peak, a plane was arriving every three minutes and around 4000 tonnes of supplies were delivered every day.
- On 15 April 1949, nearly 12,000 tonnes of coal were delivered in what became known as the 'Easter Parade'.
- Tensions remained high throughout this period and war seemed a real possibility – neither side was willing to back down.
- On 12 May, Stalin gave in and ended the blockade.

The consequences

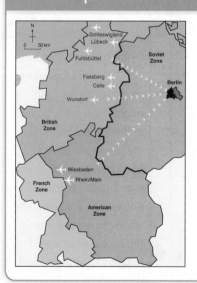

- The blockades and airlift had pushed the two sides to the brink of war and East-West relations were the worst they had ever been. Berlin remained a key location for the remainder of the Cold War.
- On 23 May 1949, West Germany became the **Federal Republic of Germany** (FDR), an independent democratic country.
- In October 1949, the **German Democratic Republic** (GDR) was created as a Soviet-style communist state.
- In April 1949, the USA, Britain and 10 other non-communist countries formed the **North Atlantic Treaty Organisation** (NATO). The USA was committed to supporting and protecting Western Europe. A Soviet rival, the **Warsaw Pact**, was created six years later.

SUMMARY

- Tensions began to increase after the Second World War due to Soviet expansion, the Long Telegram and Winston Churchill's Iron Curtain speech.

- The Truman Doctrine (1947) promised that the USA would support any country under threat from communism.

- The Marshall Plan (1947) provided American aid to rebuild Europe. Countries behind the Iron Curtain turned the aid down.

- Stalin saw American action as 'dollar imperialism' and created Cominform and Comecon in response.

- In 1948, the USSR blockaded West Berlin. The USA and Britain responded with an airlift. This represented a moment of very high tension and could have led to war.

APPLY

WRITE AN ACCOUNT

a   Create a timeline of events in Berlin from March 1948 to October 1949.

b   Write an account of how the events in Berlin led to an international crisis in 1948–1949.

EXAMINER TIP

For this question you need to refer to the Berlin Blockade and Airlift and explain the causes and consequences of these events. These then need to be related to relations between the superpowers.

REVIEW

You may want to look back at Chapter 1 to remind yourself about the division of Berlin after the Second World War.

SOURCE ANALYSIS

▼ SOURCE A   *A 1948 cartoon by the American artist D. R. Fitzpatrick; Russia is often depicted as a bear.*

a   Source A is critical of the actions of the USSR. How do you know? Explain your answer using Source A and your contextual knowledge.

EXAMINER TIP

Make sure you examine the source carefully. What does the bear represent? What is it doing? What does this action represent?

The significance of events in Asia for superpower relations

RECAP

The Communist revolution in China, 1949

Having fought a brutal civil war, Mao Tse-tung declared the establishment of the People's Republic of China on 1 October 1949. The **Nationalists**, who had previously ruled the country, retreated to the island of Taiwan. The most populous country in the world had become communist.

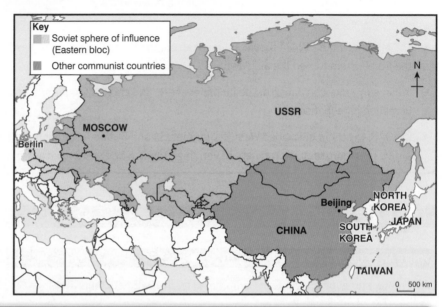

China and the USSR

Stalin immediately recognised Mao and the Communists as the rightful government of China and a **Treaty of Friendship** was signed by the two nations. It said:

- $300 million in aid would be sent to China. 95 per cent of this would need to be repaid (at a high rate of interest) and most of it had to be spent on Soviet goods.
- 8000 Chinese students could travel to the USSR to study science and technology.
- 20,000 Soviet experts were sent to help the development of China. Much of their advice seemed to benefit the USSR, rather than China.
- China agreed to give two of its major ports to the USSR and to give the Soviets the right to mine in its Xinjiang territory.

Stalin saw himself as the leader of world communism, but China was not going be like the communist countries of Eastern Europe. Unlike in the Russian Revolution, which had been led by factory workers in the cities, Chinese communists were largely peasant farmers. Although the relationship between the countries started well, it soon began to break down, particularly after Stalin's death.

China and the West

In the West, the communist takeover was seen as a disaster. The West refused even to recognise the new government, arguing instead that the government in Taiwan should be seen as the rightful rulers. In Washington and other Western capitals, Mao's victory was seen as:

- a failure of the Truman Doctrine and the policy of containment
- a victory for Stalin, who now had influence over the most highly populated country in the world
- a threat to the rest of Asia, particularly Taiwan (the last part of China held by the Nationalists) and Japan (still recovering from the effects of the Second World War).

In response to Mao's victory, the USA dramatically increased funding to Japan, and other countries in Asia, to try to combat the threat of communism in those countries. In September 1949, the highly secret National Security Council Resolution 68 (**NSC-68**) allowed for a major build-up of the American military.

REVISION SKILLS

Create a 10-point fact test to test detailed knowledge about a topic. You can swap the test with a friend.

 **APPLY**

SOURCE ANALYSIS

▼ **SOURCE A** *A cartoon by Herblock, published in the* Washington Post, *on 2 February 1951. The cartoon's caption is, 'Always glad to lend my neighbour a shovel.'*

a Study **Source A**. What does this source suggest about China? What role does it suggest Stalin had?

b   Study **Source A**. **Source A** is critical of the USSR. How do you know? Explain your answer using **Source A** and your contextual knowledge.

 EXAMINER TIP

Remember to look carefully at the details of the source. Who are the figures? What are they doing? What point is the cartoonist making? Remember to link your answer to your own knowledge. What do you know about these events that would support the cartoonist's view?

HOW FAR DO YOU AGREE?

a Create a mind-map using the information on these pages. You should include: what happened in China; the Soviet response; and the Western response.

b In no more than 50 words, summarise what made the Chinese revolution important to relations between East and West in 1949.

c   'The main reason for increased tension between East and West in Asia between 1950 and 1963 was the communist takeover in China.' How far do you agree with this statement? Explain your answer.

 EXAMINER TIP

The information in this section will help you to show how the communist takeover in China led to increased tension between East and West, but in order to decide whether this was the *main* reason for increased tension, you will need to consider other reasons in your answer. Add to your answer once you have read pages 28–31 about Korea and Vietnam.

The Korean War 1950–53

Rising tensions

- The division of Korea, along the 38th Parallel, had been agreed at the Potsdam Conference.
- Communist North Korea was led by Kim Il Sung, a Soviet-trained politician.
- South Korea was led by the American-backed Syngman Rhee, a committed anti-communist.
- Both men hoped to unite Korea under their leadership. Rhee called for American support in overthrowing Kim. Kim sent raiding parties across the border to try to undermine the southern government.

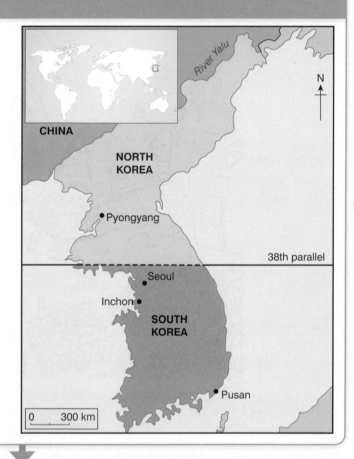

Invasion!

- In 1949, Kim asked Stalin to help him invade the South. In 1950, Stalin agreed to provide weapons and equipment, but not troops.
- The USA already had 7500 troops stationed in the South.
- In June 1950, North Korean troops invaded South Korea.

The United Nations

- In response to the North's invasion, the USA asked the UN to call for a ceasefire.
- With the USSR **boycotting** the UN and therefore unable to oppose the motion, the UN voted for the immediate withdrawal of North Korean troops.
- The North's troops remained and so the UN sent troops to support Rhee's government.
- Although the vast majority of the troops were American, they were officially UN soldiers and the USA could not be accused of acting alone.

The war

- In September 1950, USA-led forces, under the command of General MacArthur, landed at Inchon and drove the North Koreans back to the 38th Parallel.
- In October, Chinese troops helped to push the Americans back. They took control of the South Korean capital, Seoul.
- In April 1951, General MacArthur was dismissed after calling for the use of a nuclear weapon.
- By June, the war had reached stalemate and, in July, a final ceasefire was agreed, with North and South divided in almost exactly the same place as when the war started.

The consequences

- The Korean War showed that the USA was willing to go to war in order to contain communism.
- It showed the power the USA had with the UN.
- It became the first **proxy war** of the Cold War, an indirect fight between the Soviets and the Americans (the Soviets provided most of the North's weapons).
- The dismissal of MacArthur showed the USA did not want direct conflict with the USSR or to use nuclear weapons.
- The USSR was equally keen to avoid direct conflict with the USA.

REVIEW

Look at pages 36–37 to remind yourself about the role of nuclear weapons in the Cold War.

 APPLY

WRITE AN ACCOUNT

a   Create a storyboard of the key moments of the Korean War. You might include:

- the division of Korea and its two leaders
- Kim asking Stalin for weapons
- the invasion by North Korea
- the UN invasion
- Chinese involvement
- the ceasefire.

b   **EXAM QUESTION** Write an account of how the Korean War became an international crisis.

EXAMINER TIP

For this question, you need to give a detailed account of events in Korea and then place it in the wider context of East-West relations. Make sure you do both these things and don't only write about what happened in Korea. You might find it helpful to plan by listing the events in Korea and noting down their effect on East-West relations.

The Vietnam War

Indochina was a French colony, but after the Second World War many of those who lived in Indochina did not want the French back to rule them.

Indochina

- The most popular rebels in Vietnam (part of Indochina) were the **Viet Minh**, led by Ho Chi Minh.
- In 1945, he declared independence from France and established the Democratic Republic of Vietnam.
- France resisted but withdrew from Vietnam after defeat at the Battle of Dien Bien Phu in 1954.
- The new US president, Dwight D. Eisenhower, was concerned Vietnam could fall to communism.
- In July 1954, Vietnam was temporarily split in two until elections could be held: the French left the North and the Viet Minh left the South.

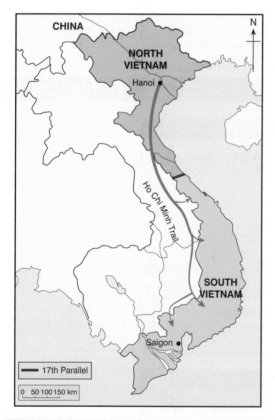

American involvement in Vietnam

- In the early 1950s, the US government devised the **Domino Theory**. It thought that if South Vietnam fell to communism, the **ideology** would spread to nearby countries. This spread would continue until Asia was entirely communist. Countries would fall like dominoes.
- To avoid conflict and growing stocks of nuclear weapons, Eisenhower established the **New Look** policy. He sent money, equipment and military and political experts to South Vietnam to help the country become secure.
- Despite the corruption and brutality of South Vietnam's anti-communist leader, Ngo Dinh Diem, the USA supported him.

The Vietcong and increasing US involvement

- In December 1960, the National Front for the Liberation of South Vietnam (the **Vietcong**) was established. Its aim was to overthrow Diem.
- The Ho Chi Minh trail was established to get weapons and equipment to the rebels from North Vietnam.
- In 1960, the new US president, John F. Kennedy, began sending over 16,000 advisors and experts to South Vietnam.
- The USA secretly backed the assassination of Diem by his opponents on 2 November 1963. It was hoped that a new leader would improve the situation.
- Kennedy himself was assassinated less than a month later. His successor, Lyndon B. Johnson, ordered full US military involvement in Vietnam. The Vietnam War would last for over a decade and cost thousands of lives.

SUMMARY

- China became communist in 1949.
- The Korean War was the first proxy war and the first actual conflict of the Cold War.
- The Vietnam War demonstrated the USA's belief in the Domino Theory and its commitment to containing communism.
- The 1950s saw the focus on the Cold War move from Europe to Asia.

⚙ APPLY

SOURCE ANALYSIS

▼ **SOURCE A** *A comment made by Eisenhower at a press conference in 1954 when asked why Indochina was important:*

You have a row of dominoes set up, you knock over the first one and what will happen to the last one is the certainty that it will go over very quickly. So you could have the beginning of a disintegration that would have the most profound influences. It takes away the so-called island defensive chain of Japan, Formosa Taiwan, of the Philippines and to the southward; it moves in to threaten Australia and New Zealand.

▶ **SOURCE B** *A comic book cover from 1960, published for American Catholic students.*

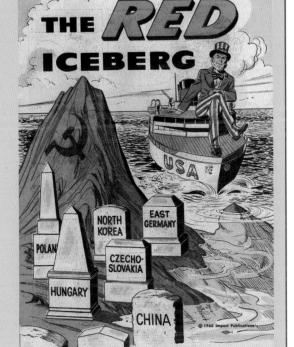

a Study **Source A**. What does the source suggest about why the USA saw Vietnam as important?

b Who is the source by? Does this make it more or less useful for understanding American policy in Vietnam?

c Now look at **Source B**. What does this source suggest about the reasons for USA involvement in Vietnam? How do you know?

d Study **Sources A** and **B**. How useful are these to a historian studying the reasons for USA involvement in Vietnam? Explain your answer using **Sources A** and **B** and your contextual knowledge.

EXAMINER TIP 🎯

Remember to consider both the content and the provenance of the sources in your answer – and to ensure you refer to both Source A and Source B.

WRITE AN ACCOUNT

a Draw a large spiral on a piece of paper. In the centre, write 'Full American military involvement'. Now go back to the outside, and add the developments that built towards US soldiers arriving in Vietnam. There is an example given to help you:

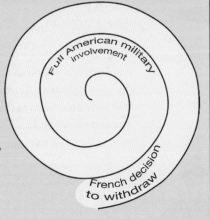

b Do you think there was a point at which US involvement became inevitable? When was it? Why?

c Write an account of how the USA became increasingly involved in the Vietnam War.

EXAMINER TIP

Remember to go beyond the specifics of Vietnam. You need to consider the USA's belief in the Domino Theory.

CHAPTER 4

Military rivalries

 **RECAP**

NATO and the Warsaw Pact

After the Second World War, many countries wanted to secure their future against possible military conflict. Alliances and treaties were two ways of achieving this. The USA and its allies formed NATO – the North Atlantic Treaty Organisation – and the USSR created the Warsaw Pact.

		NATO	The Warsaw Pact
Formed		April 1949, in response to the Berlin Blockade and Airlift.	1955, in response to West Germany being allowed to join NATO.
Membership		12 original members: USA, Canada, Britain, France, Denmark, Italy, Norway, Belgium, the Netherlands, Portugal, Luxembourg and Iceland. West Germany joined in 1955.	8 members: USSR, Bulgaria, Romania, Albania, East Germany, Poland, Hungary, Czechoslovakia.
Purpose		Collective defence and military strategy. The principle was that if one member came under attack, it would be seen as an attack on all members.	Formed as a counter-balance to the power of NATO and to protect the security and interests of countries behind the Iron Curtain.
Capabilities		Approximately 50 divisions (of which 25 were active). In 1952, it was agreed to dramatically increase the strength of NATO forces.	Approximately 5.5 million personnel in 175 divisions, 35,000 tanks and at least 100,000 aircraft.
Nuclear weapons		Held by the USA, Britain (from 1952) and France (from 1960).	Held by the USSR.
Leadership		A collective leadership of the member countries. However, the USA provided the majority of funds and fire power and built bases across Western Europe.	Officially a collective organisation like NATO, but in reality all armed forces were controlled by the USSR and all decisions were made in Moscow.

 **APPLY**

SOURCE ANALYSIS

▼ **SOURCE A** *This David Low cartoon was published two days after the signing of the North Atlantic Treaty in April 1949.*

"YOUR PLAY, JOE"

ATLANTIC PACT

a Study **Source A**. What is happening in this source? Describe it in your own words.

b What point do you think it is making?

c Do you think it is useful for understanding the situation in 1949? Include your own knowledge in your answer.

d **EXAM QUESTION** Study **Source A**. **Source A** supports NATO. How do you know? Explain your answer using **Source A** and your contextual knowledge.

WRITE AN ACCOUNT

a Create a set of revision cards. On one side write a fact about NATO, on the other side record the equivalent information about the Warsaw Pact. For example: NATO: Founded in 1949. Warsaw Pact: Founded in 1955.

b Make a list of the reasons for the formation of NATO and the Warsaw Pact.

c **EXAM QUESTION** Write an account of how the formation of NATO and the Warsaw Pact created tension between East and West.

 REVIEW ↻

You may need to look back at Chapters 1 and 2 to remind yourself about the situation in Europe upto 1949.

EXAMINER TIP ◎

For this question you will need to consider events after the formation of NATO. Why did the Treaty cause tension? How did it lead to the creation of the Warsaw Pact?

The space race

The period between the late 1950s and early 1970s saw rapid technological and scientific advancement in space exploration. In the context of the Cold War, it was a race for superiority between the USA and the USSR.

Timeline: The space race

▼ 4 October 1957

■ The USSR sends the first manmade satellite to orbit Earth: **Sputnik**. The Americans had been working on the same thing and the Soviet victory was seen as a triumph for communism.

▼ 3 November 1957

■ The USSR sends the first animal into space, a dog named Laika. The Americans scramble to catch up.

▼ 18 December 1958

■ The USA launches the first communications satellite into space.

▼ 12 April 1961

■ The USSR wins the race to send a human into space with cosmonaut Yuri Gagarin.

▼ 5 May 1961

■ The first successful American space flight, controlled by the pilot, Alan Shepard.

▼ 25 May 1961

■ President Kennedy announces that, by the end of the decade, an American will land on the moon. His promise seems impossible at the time as technology was a long way from being able to achieve this.

▼ 16 June 1963

■ First woman in space: Valentina Tereshkova from the USSR.

▼ 20 July 1969

■ Kennedy's promise is fulfilled when Neil Armstrong becomes the first human being to walk on the moon.

▼ 23 April 1971

■ First human-crewed space station is launched by the USSR.

▼ 15 July 1975

■ The first joint space mission between the USA and the USSR: **Apollo-Soyuz**. It is seen as a symbol of a new age of co-operation between the superpowers.

Why was there a space race?

The space race between the USSR and the USA developed for two main reasons:

- Propaganda – both countries were keen to show that they were superior and wanted to be seen as leading the world into the modern age.
- Weapons development – the Americans were concerned that nuclear missiles could be launched using the same system as the Soviets used to launch rockets into space. Their concern was justified: intercontinental ballistic missiles (ICBMs) could be carried thousands of miles using rockets.

APPLY

WRITE AN ACCOUNT

a Copy out a large version of this graph:

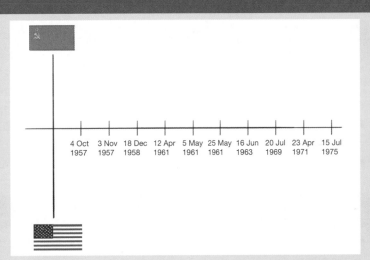

4 Oct 1957 3 Nov 1957 18 Dec 1958 12 Apr 1961 5 May 1961 25 May 1961 16 Jun 1963 20 Jul 1969 23 Apr 1971 15 Jul 1975

b Plot the key developments from the timeline on your graph. Place events that were good for the Soviets at the top, and events that were good for the Americans near the bottom. When you have finished, connect the events with a line.

c What do you notice about the line? Is one country in the lead throughout, or does it change? Who do you think 'won' the space race?

d EXAM QUESTION Write an account of how the space race changed from competition to co-operation.

EXAMINER TIP

Remember to explain the reason for developments; don't just tell the story.

REVIEW

You may want to look at the other chapters of this revision guide to remind yourself of the wider context of each development in the space race.

SOURCE ANALYSIS

a Study **Source A**. What does this source tell you about the USA's motivations in the space race?

b Can you place the source in historical context using your own knowledge? Use the timeline to help you.

c Now look at **Source B**. What does this source tell you about the space race? Can you explain the point that the cartoon is making?

d EXAM QUESTION Study **Sources A** and **B**. How useful are these to a historian studying the space race? Explain your answer using **Sources A** and **B** and your contextual knowledge.

▼ **SOURCE A** *From a memo to President Kennedy from Vice President Johnson, 28 April 1961:*

> This country should be realistic and recognise that other nations, regardless of their appreciation of our idealistic values, will tend to align themselves with the country which they believe will be the world leader – the winner in the long run. Dramatic accomplishments in Space are being increasingly identified as a major indicator of world leadership.

▼ **SOURCE B** *An Australian cartoon from April 1961. The caption said, 'Next time, Comrade Gagarin, wear these red-coloured glasses!'*

EXAMINER TIP

Remember to look out for a common idea that both sources might share and that you can talk about.

 **RECAP**

The arms race

The development of nuclear weaponry

- The use of atomic bombs against Japan in 1945 led to an increase in tension between the superpowers and started a nuclear arms race between them.
- The Soviets successfully detonated their first A-bomb on 29 August 1949.
- The Americans responded by building the **hydrogen bomb** in 1952. The Soviets had built their own within a year.
- Defence budgets rose on both sides as more and more weapons were developed.

Mutually Assured Destruction and Brinkmanship

- Within a few years, both the USSR and the USA had the ability to totally obliterate the other.
- By 1960, the Americans had nuclear missiles that could be fired from land, sea and air, including Polaris, a missile that could be launched from a submarine.
- The knowledge that launching a weapon would lead to retaliation and therefore the destruction of both sides was known as **Mutually Assured Destruction** (MAD). This is probably the main reason no nuclear weapons were ever launched.
- MAD did not mean that nuclear war did not come close on a number of occasions. From the 1950s onwards, any moment of tension brought the fear of nuclear war. Each side would push the other to the brink of using weapons, knowing that they would eventually back down. This was known as **brinkmanship**.
- The Berlin Blockade and the Korean War both raised the possibility of nuclear weapons being used, but it was during the Cuban Missile Crisis, in 1962, that the world came closest to destruction. After the crisis, the two sides began to discuss reducing their nuclear arsenals and a direct phoneline between the White House and the Kremlin was created.

> **REVIEW** ⟳
>
> Look at pages 48–49 to remind yourself about the events of the Cuban Missile Crisis.

Preparation for nuclear attack

Governments on both sides made preparations for a nuclear war. These ranged from the construction of huge underground bunkers to campaigns to teach children to 'duck and cover' under their school desks. While the bunkers were a serious measure to ensure government could continue to operate, many of the public awareness campaigns were simply attempts to reassure people and prevent panic.

The impact of the arms race

'Ban the bomb' movement

From the 1950s, some people questioned whether nuclear weapons were morally right. The Campaign for Nuclear Disarmament (CND) called for Britain to **unilaterally disarm**. Similar movements grew across the Western world.

The bomb in popular culture

The nuclear standoff between East and West inspired many works of literature, film and television. One of the most famous is the satirical film *Dr. Strangelove*, which tells the story of an accidental nuclear strike by the USA and the automatic retaliation by the USSR's doomsday machine. The film points out the danger and the absurdity of the situation.

SUMMARY

- NATO (1949) and the Warsaw Pact (1955) were created as powerful alliances to stand opposed to each other in Europe.

- The space race was motivated by the need for propaganda and as a way to develop technology that could be used for weapons.

- The arms race saw a huge escalation in the number of weapons that each side possessed.

- The arms race led to MAD and brinkmanship. It also had a huge impact on the societies of both sides.

 **APPLY**

HOW FAR DO YOU AGREE?

a   Create a mind-map showing the key features of the nuclear arms race.

b
> **EXAM QUESTION** 'The nuclear arms race was the main consequence of superpower rivalry between 1945 and 1965.' How far do you agree with this statement? Explain your answer.

_____

_____

_____

_____

_____

_____

_____

_____

_____

_____

_____

_____

_____

 EXAMINER TIP

Think about the reasons for the nuclear arms race – was it simply about mistrust or were there other reasons? You may want to look at other points of tension between East and West during the Cold War, such as the space race and the conflicts in Asia.

WRITE AN ACCOUNT

a   Create a timeline of the key moments in the nuclear arms race. You should include:

- the development of particular weapons technology
- key moments of brinkmanship
- treaties that were signed towards the end of the 1960s and the beginning of the 1970s.

b   Colour-code the timeline showing the three categories.

CHAPTER 5 · The 'thaw'

 **RECAP**

The Hungarian Uprising, 1956

Hungary before the uprising

- After the Second World War, Hungary fell within the Soviet sphere of influence and elections were tightly controlled to ensure communists came to power.
- From 1949, the leader was Mátyás Rákosi, a hard-line Stalinist who did not tolerate any opposition. The secret police helped him to keep a firm grip on the country. Many Hungarians began to resent the brutality of Rákosi and the tight control of Moscow.
- Hungary was a strongly Catholic country and the arrest of Cardinal Mindszenty and other religious leaders caused particular anger.
- Following Stalin's death in February 1956, new Soviet leader Nikita Khrushchev criticised Stalin's brutality and suggested a more open and peaceful approach from the government. This process was known as '**de-Stalinisation**'.
- Students in Hungary saw this as an opportunity to bring change to the country and gain greater independence from Moscow.

The Uprising

- 23 October 1956, students took to the streets of the Hungarian capital, Budapest. They issued a list of demands that included:
    - greater freedoms and **civil rights**
    - the removal of Rákosi and the return of the exiled Imre Nagy, a communist who supported reform
    - the withdrawal of Soviet troops.
- The small protests grew quickly and violence began to spread. Soviet tanks were set alight and, in response, some fired on the protesters.
- Nagy called for calm and pledged support for the Hungarian Communist Party. Keen to avoid violence, Khrushchev ordered the withdrawal of Soviet troops from the country between 29 and 31 October, and the protesters celebrated a great victory.

A new Hungary?

- With Soviet tanks gone, and Nagy as prime minster, it seemed that life in the country would improve.
- Protesters called for even greater reforms and Nagy agreed to withdraw from the Warsaw Pact. On 1 November 1956, he announced that Hungary was now an independent and **neutral** country.

The Soviet response

- Although Khrushchev had been willing to give some ground, Nagy's decision to leave the Warsaw Pact went too far. He was worried that other members might be inspired to follow Hungary's example.
- On 4 November, Soviet tanks entered the country and quickly overpowered the Hungarians. The uprising was crushed.
- Nagy was forced from power and later tried and executed. He was replaced by János Kádár, who dealt brutally with any opposition and was totally loyal to Moscow.

The West's response

- Although many Hungarians believed that the USA would come to their aid, President Eisenhower was clear: Hungary was within the Soviet **sphere of influence** and any American interference risked direct conflict with Moscow.
- The United Nations discussed the issue of Hungary on 4 November. The Security Council held a vote calling the USSR to withdraw, but the USSR simply **vetoed** it. Although the General Assembly condemned the USSR's actions, it could do nothing to stop them.
- For most countries, the Suez Crisis was of much more concern than events in Hungary.

The effects on the Cold War

Despite his calls for **peaceful co-existence** between East and West and the process of de-Stalinisation in the USSR, Khrushchev had shown that he was willing to do anything to keep countries under Moscow's control.

The USA, on the other hand, had established that it would not interfere in events behind the Iron Curtain.

APPLY

WRITE AN ACCOUNT

a Create a story board that tells the story of the Hungarian Uprising and the USSR's response.

b **EXAM QUESTION** Write an account of how events in Hungary became an international crisis during 1956.

HOW FAR DO YOU AGREE ?

a Make a list of the reasons for Khrushchev's decision to send tanks into Hungary.

b **EXAM QUESTION** 'The Soviet response to the Hungarian Uprising meant that tensions remained high between the superpowers between 1950 and 1960.' How far do you agree with this statement? Explain your answer.

EXAMINER TIP

This question requires you to place the events in Hungary in 1956 into a wider Cold War context. You need to structure your answer to explain how one event led to another. To achieve the higher marks make sure you explain what the impact of these events was at an international level.

EXAMINER TIP

Consider what other events could be set against the Hungarian Uprising as reasons why tensions remained high. Don't overlook the dates given in the question either – think about what happened during the *whole* time period mentioned.

The U2 Crisis and the Paris Peace Summit, 1960

Fear of communism increased among ordinary US citizens and within US politics during the 1950s and 1960s. The thaw in relations between the USA and the USSR came to an abrupt end when the Soviets shot down an American spy plane.

- The U2 spy planes were the USA's most effective method of gathering intelligence. They flew at a height of 23,000 metres and were able to photograph weapons development without detection.
- This was until the plane flown by US pilot Gary Powers was shot down by the USSR's new, more powerful, anti-aircraft guns on 1 May 1960.
- The Americans claimed that it was simply a weather plane that had strayed into Soviet territory, but there was clear evidence that this was not the case.
- Powers was eventually put on trial and sentenced to ten years' imprisonment.

The immediate consequences: a failed peace summit

- A day after claiming that it was a weather plane, the US government admitted that it was a spy plane. President Eisenhower refused to apologise.
- Eisenhower and Khrushchev were due to meet at the long-planned **Paris Peace Summit** in May 1960. The **U2 Crisis** completely overshadowed the event.
- Khrushchev was highly critical of Eisenhower, describing him as a 'thief caught red-handed in his theft'. He walked out of the summit before any discussions could take place.
- Khrushchev cancelled what was due to be a historic trip by the US president to the USSR in June.
- Eisenhower promised only to 'suspend' spy flights and Khrushchev refused to meet the president again.

The wider consequences

- The Paris Peace Summit was supposed to represent a step towards improved relations and to build on Khrushchev's call for 'peaceful co-existence' between East and West. Eisenhower hoped to end his presidency by improving the USA's relationship with the USSR. Instead, tensions were higher than ever.
- On the surface, the growth in tension seemed to be entirely the fault of the Americans. However, some have argued that Khrushchev wanted the summit to fail to show his political opponents in Moscow that he was a tough leader on the world stage.

The fear of spies in the USA

While tensions were running high abroad, the USA was itself in a growing state of fear about communism at home. Throughout the 1950s, Senator Joseph McCarthy led a campaign to root out communism in the USA, while the **House Un-American Activities Committee** (HUAC) investigated anyone with the slightest suspicion of links to communism. People began to believe that there were indeed 'reds under the bed'.

Most of those accused were innocent but, in 1950, a State Department official, Alger Hiss, was found to have passed secrets to the USSR. Julius and Ethel Rosenberg were also executed for being Soviet spies.

SUMMARY

- The Hungarian Uprising was a response to de-Stalinisation and Khrushchev's promise of a new approach.

- Imre Nagy led the reforms in Hungary, which included greater freedoms and leaving the Warsaw Pact.

- The USSR sent tanks to end the Hungarian Uprising; the West did not interfere.

- The shooting down of the U2 spy plane in 1960 led to the failure of the Paris Peace Summit.

- When Eisenhower left office at the beginning of 1961, tensions between East and West were extremely high.

 APPLY

SOURCE ANALYSIS

▼ **SOURCE A** *An American cartoon depicting the events at the Paris Peace Summit, entitled 'Better relations through trade'; it appeared in the Hartford Times on 14 February 1962.*

a   Study **Source A**. What events do you think this source is referring to? What evidence do you have for this?

b

> **EXAM QUESTION** Study **Source A**. **Source A** suggests that the main reason for the failure of the Paris Peace Summit was the U2 Crisis. How do you know?
>
> Explain your answer using **Source A** and your contextual knowledge.

EXAMINER TIP

Remember to refer to all of the details of the source, including the figures at the bottom. Artists draft their cartoons carefully and even the smallest detail can have significant meaning.

EXAMINER TIP

Remember to consider all of the possible reasons for the summit's failure, including the U2 incident itself and Khrushchev's behaviour at the summit. You should not limit yourself to discussing only the reason given in the statement; an examiner will expect to see a wider understanding of several possible reasons.

HOW FAR DO YOU AGREE?

a   Create a flow chart that shows the events leading up to the failure of the Paris Peace Summit. You might wish to include: the shooting down of the U2 spy plane; the USA's claim that it was a weather plane; the USA admitting that it was a spy plane; Eisenhower refusing to apologise; and Khrushchev storming out of the meeting.

b

> **EXAM QUESTION** 'The main reason why there was no improvement in superpower relations between 1956 and 1960 was because of Soviet actions.' How far do you agree with this statement? Explain your answer.

The Berlin Wall

The Berlin problem

- Berlin had been divided since 1945: the USSR controlled East Berlin while the West became an island of capitalism behind the Iron Curtain. The USSR saw West Berlin as an embarrassment, while the West saw it as a strategic and symbolic victory.
- The city had been at the centre of some of the Cold War's biggest moments of tension, most notably the blockade and airlift of 1948–49.
- While citizens of West Berlin enjoyed freedom and luxuries, their eastern neighbours lived in a tightly controlled state.
- Many East Berliners took the opportunity to defect to the West by crossing the border. Once in the western sector, they could travel freely to West Germany. By 1961, thousands were crossing every day.

REVIEW

Look at pages 24–25 to remind yourself about the Berlin Blockade and Airlift.

The Vienna Summit, 3–4 June 1961

When the new US president, John F. Kennedy, met with Khrushchev in Vienna, it was an opportunity to repair the relations damaged by the U2 Crisis and the Paris Peace Summit. Khrushchev dominated the discussions, and seemed not to take the young and inexperienced Kennedy seriously.

The Berlin Wall

- With thousands defecting from East Berlin to West Berlin every day, something had to be done. On 13 August 1961, East German troops closed the border and stopped anyone from crossing.
- Within a few hours, barbed wire fences were put up and trains were stopped from crossing the border. The fences zigzagged through the middle of the city, dividing streets, and even buildings.
- Over the following week, the fence was replaced by a concrete wall that would remain in place for nearly 30 years.
- The official reason given for the wall was that it was to stop Western spies from entering Soviet territory but, in reality, it was to stop the many educated people who were leaving East Berlin. It also prevented East Berliners from seeing what life was like in West Berlin.

 **APPLY**

SOURCE ANALYSIS

▼ **SOURCE A** *Adapted from the transcript of Krushchev's words in a meeting between him and the leader of East Germany on 1 August 1961:*

> Many educated people, scientists and engineers, have fled the GDR. Something must be done to stop this loss of key people. We think that the current tensions with the West present a good opportunity to place an iron ring around Berlin. We can explain it because we feel threatened with war and want to keep out spies. The Germans will understand this explanation. Russian troops should man the ring but your troops should control the checkpoints. This must happen before the conclusion of a peace treaty so that we can use it as a bargaining tool and show that we mean business. If we are forced to war, then there will be war.

▶ **SOURCE B**

An American cartoon by Don Wright, published in the Miami Herald *in 1961; the figure talking on the wall is Khrushchev.*

a What does **Source A** suggest were the reasons for the building of the Berlin Wall? Highlight them on the source.

b What does **Source B** suggest was the reason for the building of the Berlin Wall? How far does it match what is said in **Source A**?

c
 EXAM QUESTION   Study **Sources A** and **B**. How useful are **Sources A** and **B** to a historian studying the building of the Berlin Wall in 1961? Explain your answer using **Sources A** and **B** and your contextual knowledge.

EXAMINER TIP

First, use the content of each source, linked to your own knowledge, to explain what it tells us about why the Berlin Wall was built. Then use the provenance to work out how useful the sources are. You should assume that the sources are useful – your discussion should focus on what useful things each one tells you.

Kennedy and Berlin

A young president

When John F. Kennedy became US president in January 1961, he was 30 years younger than his predecessor. Many Americans saw him as a break with the past and as representing a more optimistic view of the future. His critics saw him as far too inexperienced on the world stage and the first few months of his presidency, with the Vienna Summit and the building of the Berlin Wall, seemed to confirm these fears.

Another crisis in Berlin

In October 1961, there was another moment of tension when an American diplomat was refused entry to East Berlin. The incident led to a stand off at the border, which included tanks. The crisis was averted when Kennedy and Khrushchev both agreed to withdraw. The two sides took turns reversing their tanks 5 metres at a time. The slightest error could have led to war.

Kennedy's response to the wall

Kennedy was angered by the wall's construction, but he was also practical. As long as West Berlin remained free, East Berlin was not worth a war.

In June 1963, he travelled to West Berlin where he visited the wall and looked over into the East. It was a highly symbolic visit to the very centre of the Cold War. The speech he gave there made clear that the USA remained committed to fighting communism, using Berlin as an example and proclaiming, 'Ich bin ein Berliner' (I am a Berliner).

SUMMARY

- Tensions between the superpowers in 1961 remained high and little was achieved at the Vienna Summit.
- There was a crisis in East Berlin over the number of people defecting to the West through West Berlin.
- On 13 August 1961, the border was closed. Moscow and the East German government claimed this was to stop Western spies, but in reality it was to halt the flow of refugees fleeing to the West.
- Kennedy was angered by the wall but unwilling to go to war over it.
- He visited West Berlin in June 1963 and made a speech in which he reiterated the USA's commitment to fighting communism.
- The Berlin Wall showed that tensions remained high, but it did settle the matter of Berlin, at least for the time being.

⚙ APPLY

HOW FAR DO YOU AGREE?

a Make a list of the ways in which the building of the Berlin Wall led to tension between the superpowers.

_____

_____

_____

_____

b Now make a list of ways in which it did not lead to tension.

_____

_____

_____

_____

c **EXAM QUESTION** 'The construction of the Berlin Wall created great tension between East and West between 1961 and 1963.' How far do you agree with this statement? Explain your answer.

> **EXAMINER TIP** 🎯
>
> The question gives you specific dates to consider. Remember, your answer should only refer to events and developments between these dates.

CHAPTER 7

Tensions over Cuba

 **RECAP**

Castro's revolution

Batista vs Castro

- Between 1933 and 1959, Cuba was ruled by a corrupt and brutal government led by Batista.
- American investment had enabled many members of the Cuban government and US businessmen to become very wealthy, but life for ordinary Cubans was tough.
- By the 1950s, many Cubans were fed up with Batista's regime and a young lawyer named Fidel Castro called for a revolution. He was arrested and sent into exile.
- Castro returned to Cuba, with 81 supporters, in 1956 and began a two-year guerrilla war campaign against the government. His support grew.
- On 1 January 1959, Batista's government collapsed and Castro declared a new Cuba.

Castro's Cuba

- Although he and his supporters were left wing, Castro never referred to communism. Instead he talked of a fight by ordinary Cubans for a fairer and freer society.
- Castro visited the USA shortly after coming to power. He said he was willing to work with the Americans, but President Eisenhower refused to meet with him.
- In Cuba, Castro began reorganising the way the country worked, taking businesses and industry into state ownership (including a number of American businesses).
- With the USA unwilling to work with him, Castro turned to the USSR for help in building Cuba's economy. In response, the USA placed an **embargo** on the country (a total ban on trade). Cuba was now totally reliant on the USSR.

The Bay of Pigs, 1961

With an ally of the USSR on the USA's doorstep, the CIA (America's foreign intelligence service) began to draw up a plan to help Castro's exiled opponents retake Cuba. When Kennedy took office in January 1961, he gave the plan the go ahead.

The plan

A large group of Cuban exiles, trained by the CIA, would take control of Cuba. The US Air Force would give them support. The assumption was that the invasion would inspire other Cubans to take up arms against Castro.

The problems begin

Shortly before the plan was put into action, it became clear that most Cubans supported Castro and would not join the invasion. A number of senior figures in the US government also felt that their involvement was illegal under international law.

However having spent $5 million on preparations it was decided that the plan was worth the risk.

The consequences

Despite Kennedy's late decision, it was still obvious that the USA was involved. The USA had broken international law and been completely humiliated. Kennedy, just months into his presidency, looked weak and incompetent.

Although victorious, Castro knew that the Americans would not give up and this pushed him further into his alliance with the USSR.

The invasion

On 17 April 1961, the Cuban exiles landed on the beach in the Bay of Pigs. It was a total disaster. At the last moment, Kennedy withdrew the support of the US Air Force and the exiles were left totally exposed. 200 were killed and 1197 were taken prisoner by Castro's forces. No one in Cuba came to their aid.

APPLY

SOURCE ANALYSIS

▼ **SOURCE A** *A cartoon drawn by the American cartoonist Clifford Baldowski and published in the* Atlanta Journal *newspaper in January 1959.*

RED VOODOO

a What does **Source A** show? What point is it making?

b **EXAM QUESTION** Study **Source A**. **Source A** is critical of Castro and Cuba. How do you know? Explain your answer using **Source A** and your contextual knowledge.

HOW FAR DO YOU AGREE?

a Create a timeline of events in Cuba between 1959 and 1961.

c **EXAM QUESTION** 'The increase in tensions between East and West over Cuba between 1959 and 1961 was the result of American actions.' How far do you agree with this statement? Explain your answer.

The Cuban Missile Crisis, 1962

REVIEW

The Cuban Missile Crisis is a key moment in the arms race. To remind yourself about the arms race look at pages 36–37.

Soviet missiles in Cuba

- After the Bay of Pigs incident, Castro became closer to Moscow. For Khrushchev, having an ally a few miles from the American coast was an opportunity not to be missed, especially with US bases and nuclear weapons in Turkey near the Soviet border.
- The first nuclear weapons arrived in Cuba in the summer of 1962 but it was not until **14 October** that the US realised what was going on.
- After a week of discussions with his advisors, Kennedy revealed the missiles' existence to the American people. He also ordered a blockade of Cuba, beginning on **21 October**, saying that the US Navy would fire on any ship that tried to reach the island. The following day, he placed the USA on **DEFCON 3**.

Tensions rise

- Convinced that Kennedy would invade Cuba, Khrushchev prepared for a fight.
- On **23 October**, Soviet ships approached Cuba, carrying more missiles. It was now a game of brinkmanship.
- On **24 October**, the UN Secretary General, U Thant, called for a compromise and the ships faced each other waiting for the other side to back down. The US declared DEFCON 2.

On the brink of war

- At 7:15am, on **25 October**, a Soviet ship entered the quarantine zone. It was stopped by the Americans, but allowed to pass once it was established it was an oil tanker.
- Kennedy assembled 120,000 US troops in Florida, ready for an invasion of Cuba.
- On **26 October**, Kennedy received a letter from Khrushchev saying that he would remove the missiles.

President Kennedy,
The White House,
Washington DC,
USA

Danger increases

A number of events, beyond the control of the leaders, made nuclear war seem increasingly likely:

- On **27 October**, the US Navy detected a Soviet submarine close to Cuba. When the Americans sent depth charges to force the submarine to surface, it became clear that the Soviet vessel had not had any contact with the outside world. Believing that a war had begun, the captain almost launched a nuclear torpedo.
- On the same morning, the Cubans shot down a Soviet spy plane.
- Later in the day, another American plane drifted into Soviet airspace.

Crisis averted

- Later on **27 October**, Khrushchev sent a second letter to Kennedy. Once again he promised to remove the missiles but this time also demanded the removal of US missiles from Turkey and Italy.
- Kenney agreed on the basis that the removal of US missiles would be kept secret. The crisis was over.

President Kennedy,
The White House,
Washington DC,
USA

 APPLY

SOURCE ANALYSIS

▼ **SOURCE A** *A British cartoon published on 29 October 1962.*

▼ **SOURCE B** *Written by the American journalist I. F. Stone shortly after Kennedy's assassination in 1963:*

> What if the Russians had refused to back down and remove their missiles from Cuba? What if they had called our bluff and war had begun, and escalated? How would the historians of mankind, if a fragment survived, have regarded the events of October? Since this is the kind of bluff that can easily be played once too often, and that his successors may feel urged to imitate, it would be well to think it over carefully before praising Kennedy as a champion of peace.

a Describe **Source A**. What does it show?

b What point do you think the source is making about the Cuban Missile Crisis?

c Now study **Source B**. What does this source suggest about the Cuban Missile Crisis?

d Study **Sources A** and **B**. How useful are **Sources A** and **B** to a historian studying the Cuban Missile Crisis? Explain your answer using **Sources A** and **B** and your contextual knowledge.

HOW FAR DO YOU AGREE?

a Create a timeline of the main events of the Cuban Missile Crisis. Start with when the Soviet missiles arrived in Cuba and finish with the agreement between Kennedy and Khrushchev.

b Make a list of the biggest moments of tension during the crisis. Can you explain what made them important?

c 'The main reason for the Cuban Missile Crisis was President Kennedy's actions.' How far do you agree with this statement? Explain your answer.

EXAMINER TIP

Remember for a 'how useful' question you need to examine not only the content of the sources but also any additional information you are given about the source's provenance.

EXAMINER TIP

Remember to consider all of the high-tension points and their causes in your answer. Lots of students are good at listing the different points, but not as good at explaining their impact. Make sure you link your points back to the question using a sentence like: 'This was also a high-tension point in the crisis because …'. Make sure you explain what the impact on the crisis was – how did it add to the problems?

The consequences of the Cuban Missile Crisis

There were positive and negative consequences of the Cuban Missile Crisis, for both the USSR and the USA.

Khrushchev and the USSR

✓ Publicly, Khrushchev claimed that he had agreed to remove the missiles to encourage world peace.

✓ He believed that his actions showed that the USSR was willing to support smaller countries against the USA.

✓ Cuba remained a close ally of the USSR for the remainder of the Cold War, much to the USA's frustration.

✓ The removal of American weapons from Turkey and Italy was also a major victory for Khrushchev, albeit a secret one.

✗ Senior figures within the Communist Party felt that Khrushchev had been reckless during the crisis. They also felt that he backed down just as he seemed to be gaining an advantage.

✗ Concerns over Khrushchev's handling of the crisis was one of the issues that led to his removal from power on 14 October 1964.

Results of the Cuban Missile Crisis

Superpower relations after the crisis

Kennedy and the USA

✓ Kennedy had shown that he could stand up to Khrushchev and that he was not a weak leader, silencing many of his critics.

✓ The removal of missiles from Cuba meant that there was no direct nuclear threat to the USA. Missiles were not yet powerful enough to reach the USA from the USSR.

✗ The removal of American weapons from Turkey and Italy, had it been public knowledge, would have been seen as a major retreat from Europe by the USA.

- The Cuban Missile Crisis drew attention to the risks of brinkmanship and the lack of control that the leaders actually had over events.
- The crisis was only resolved when Kennedy and Khrushchev communicated directly.
- In order to avoid a similar crisis in the future, a special phone 'hotline' was introduced between the White House and the Kremlin.
- The **Partial Test Ban Treaty** of 1963 banned the testing of nuclear weapons, except underground.
- Both sides maintained their heavy nuclear arsenals (collection of weapons) but it was recognised that the arms race could not continue in the same way.

SUMMARY

- The Cuban Revolution of 1959 brought Castro to power in Cuba. Castro's government became increasingly allied with the USSR.

- The attempt to overthrow Castro at the Bay of Pigs was a total disaster and a humiliation for President Kennedy.

- The decision by Khrushchev to station nuclear missiles on Cuba began a period of 14 days in which tensions between the USSR and the USA reached the highest point of the Cold War; nuclear war seemed likely.

- After the crisis, both sides wanted to avoid a repetition and so began efforts to reduce tensions.

 APPLY

SOURCE ANALYSIS

▼ **SOURCE A** *A cartoon by the American cartoonist Herblock, published in the Washington Post in November 1962.*

"Let's Get A Lock For This Thing"

NUCLEAR WAR

HERBLOCK

▼ **SOURCE B** *Kennedy's official statement from 28 October 1962:*

It is my earnest hope that the governments of the world can, with a solution to the Cuban crisis, turn their urgent attention to the compelling necessity for ending the arms race and reducing world tensions. This applies to the military confrontation between the Warsaw Pact and NATO countries as well as other situations in other parts of the world where tensions lead to the wasteful diversion of resources to weapons of war.

a   Look at **Source A**. What point is this source making about the Cuban Missile Crisis?

b   Now look at **Source B**. What does this source suggest about the Cuban Missile Crisis?

c
 How useful are **Sources A** and **B** to a historian studying the Cuban Missile Crisis? Explain your answer using **Sources A** and **B** and your contextual knowledge.

REVISION SKILLS

a   Create some revision cards on the following topics:
   - Castro's revolution
   - the Bay of Pigs
   - missiles in Cuba
   - the roles of Castro, Khrushchev and Kennedy
   - fears of the USA and reaction to missiles in Cuba
   - dangers and results of crisis.

EXAMINER TIP

Remember to consider the provenance of the sources. Who created them? Why? Does this change how they can be useful?

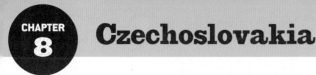

Dubček and the Prague Spring movement, 1968

As with other countries behind the Iron Curtain, Czechoslovakia was tightly controlled by Moscow:

- It was a one-party communist state.
- As a member of the Warsaw Pact it answered to Moscow.
- The press and media were tightly controlled and opposition was banned.
- There were almost no opportunities to see what life was like outside the country.

However, by the 1960s:

- Economic problems were mounting.
- The country's leader, Antonín Novotný, was corrupt and unpopular. Calls for reform were growing, most notably by the respected economist Ota Šik, who argued that ordinary people should have more power and that the ban on private businesses should be lifted.
- Moscow rejected the calls for change.

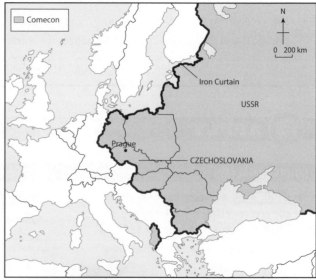

'Socialism with a human face'

In January 1968, Novotný was forced to resign by the Soviet government. He was replaced by Alexander Dubček, whom Moscow believed would calm the situation. Much to their surprise, he began introducing reforms, including:

- the removal of state controls on industry, allowing Czechs to run their own businesses
- allowing public meetings and freedom of speech
- ending press censorship
- giving Czechs the right to visit non-communist countries
- allowing the formation of **trade unions**.

Although very unhappy, Moscow allowed the reforms to stand. Moscow's acceptance of the changes encouraged Dubček to go further. He announced plans to open the borders with Western countries and remove all remaining censorship of the press. The changes in Czechoslovakia became known as the **Prague Spring**.

REVIEW ⟳

The Warsaw Pact was an important organisation in the Prague Spring. Look back at pages 32–33 to remind yourself about it.

The challenge for Brezhnev

The Prague Spring was the first major challenge for Leonid Brezhnev, the new Soviet leader. He needed to maintain control of Czechoslovakia, without causing more problems. The situation was made worse by students in Poland calling for reform to be allowed in their country. Other Warsaw Pact leaders were concerned.

As Dubček's reforms became bolder, the Warsaw Pact demanded action.

- The Pact met in June 1968. The decision was made to carry out military exercises along the Czech border. This sent a clear message to Dubček.
- In July, the Warsaw Pact met again, this time without Czechoslovakia, and issued the Warsaw Letter. This was a final warning to Dubček to back down on his reforms. The Czech leader did not listen, and the Warsaw Pact used force to solve the problem.

⚙ APPLY

SOURCE ANALYSIS

▼ **SOURCE A** *A cartoon by the British cartoonist Michael Cummings, published on 24 July 1968, in the Daily Express newspaper. It shows Dubček meeting Brezhnev and other Soviet leaders.*

" Of course, Mr. Dubcek, we've had to bring a few lady stenographers, one or two secretaries and some tea boys . . ."

a Look at **Source A**. Describe what you can see in the source. What point do you think it is making?

_____

_____

_____

_____

_____

_____

b **EXAM QUESTION** Study **Source A**. Source A is critical of the Warsaw Pact. How do you know? Explain your answer using **Source A** and your contextual knowledge.

EXAMINER TIP

Use the evidence from the source with your own knowledge about the event. Why might Dubček not trust the Warsaw Pact?

The Soviet invasion and its effects on East-West relations

On 20 August 1968, Soviet forces entered Czechoslovakia and seized control of Prague. Although there was some civilian resistance, Dubček ordered the Czech army not to resist. A hundred protesters were killed and 500 were wounded. The Prague Spring was over and a new hard-line government was installed by Moscow.

The global communist response	The Western response
• Communists around the world were outraged by the USSR's actions. • Many communists in the West saw the invasion as a betrayal of communist principles and an act of imperialism. • There were protests in Yugoslavia and China – communist countries that were not part of the Soviet sphere of influence. • There was even a small protest in Red Square, Moscow. • The biggest threat to Soviet leaders came from the Red Army. The soldiers had been told that the invasion was at the request of the Czech people. When they arrived, it was clear that this was a lie. Returning soldiers shared their experiences and this damaged the reputation of the Soviet leadership. • For many, events in Czechoslovakia destroyed their faith in communism.	• The USA condemned the invasion and cancelled a meeting between Brezhnev and President Johnson. However, the American government was much more concerned with the situation in Vietnam and wanted to avoid increased tensions with Moscow. • Other Western governments condemned the invasion and there was an attempt to pass a Resolution, or statement, at the United Nations condemning the violence. The USSR's veto made this impossible. • It had been established in Hungary, in 1956, that the West would not interfere with Soviet action behind the Iron Curtain.

The Brezhnev Doctrine

In November 1968, Brezhnev made a speech in which he made clear that if any other Warsaw Pact country behaved in the same way as Czechoslovakia had done, it would face the same consequences.

Impact in the West

At first the USA ended talks intended to improve relations with the USSR. However, it quickly decided to take a different view of the policy in order to save the progress that had been made.

Impact in the East

China regarded the Brezhnev Doctrine with suspicion; the Chinese were worried that it suggested the USSR might interfere in China, which was undergoing a cultural revolution.

SUMMARY

- Moscow responded to calls for reform in Czechoslovakia by appointing a new leader to calm the situation.
- Dubček had the opposite effect, introducing a number of reforms.
- The Warsaw Pact countries were concerned and took steps to pressurise Dubček into backing down.
- Dubček would not back down and Soviet troops invaded Czechoslovakia.
- The Brezhnev Doctrine established that any Warsaw Pact country that tried to introduce reform would suffer the same consequences as Czechoslovakia.

 APPLY

WRITE AN ACCOUNT

a Create a mind-map called 'Impact of the Prague Spring'. Include detail about: Czechoslovakia before the Prague Spring; Dubček's reforms; the Warsaw Pact's military exercises; the Warsaw Letter; the Soviet invasion.

b Write an account of how events in Czechoslovakia led to invasion by the USSR in August 1968.

 EXAMINER TIP

Remember you should refer to life in Czechoslovakia in the 1960s as a starting point for answering this question.

HOW FAR DO YOU AGREE?

a Make a list of the consequences of the Prague Spring.

_____

_____

_____

_____

b Which do you think was the most important consequence? Why?

_____

_____

_____

_____

c 'The main result of the Soviet invasion of Czechoslovakia in 1968 was to damage belief in Communism.' How far do you agree with this statement? Explain your answer.

 EXAMINER TIP

When considering 'belief in Communism', you need to think about people on both sides of the Iron Curtain, and elsewhere in the world.

CHAPTER 9

An easing of tension

RECAP

Sources of tension

By the late 1960s, both sides were keen to avoid the high levels of tension that had almost led to nuclear war. However, there remained two main issues between the superpowers:

1. **Vietnam:** The USA involvement in Vietnam had grown significantly by the end of the 1960s. The Soviets saw the USA's actions as an attempt to force its political system on an area that was embracing communism. The war finally ended in 1973. By 1975, Vietnam was entirely communist

2. **Human rights:** The lack of free speech and other human rights within the USSR and the rest of the Warsaw Pact was a source of concern for the USA. Many saw the Cold War as a struggle between freedom and oppression. Although the issue did not disappear, American leaders did not want it to stop progress when it came to peace talks and so chose not to push the issue

REVIEW

Look back at pages 30–31 to remind yourself about the situation in Vietnam.

Détente

The period from the late 1960s to the early 1970s saw an improved relationship between the USSR and the USA. There was much more dialogue between the leaders and the threat of war decreased – there was even a joint space mission!

There were four main reasons for **détente**:

REVIEW

Look back at pages 48–49 to remind yourself about the Cuban Missile Crisis

The China-Soviet split: As relations between Moscow and Beijing deteriorated, the USA seized the opportunity to build a relationship with the world's second communist power. In February 1972, Richard Nixon became the first US president to visit China.

The nuclear issue: The Cuban Missile Crisis had shown that neither side was willing to use nuclear weapons and bring about their own destruction. There was also concern that other less stable countries could develop nuclear bombs. Co-operation could help limit the spread of the technology.

Reasons for détente

The lessons of conflict: The war in Vietnam had shown that nuclear weapons did not help win conventional wars. Neither side wanted war with the other and so talking made sense.

The economic issue: Both countries were spending billions of dollars fighting the Cold War. Continuing the arms race would have bankrupted the USSR.

SALT I

The **Strategic Arms Limitation Talks** (SALT), which began in 1969, were the most serious talks that have ever taken place between the two superpowers. A number of treaties were signed that included:

- banning new ballistic missiles
- reducing the number of anti-ballistic missile defence systems that could be built.

SALT I was officially signed by Brezhnev and Nixon at the Moscow Summit of May 1972. Talks for SALT II began immediately. The improved relations did not last, however, and the Cold War continued for another 20 years with significant moments of tension, most notably in Africa, the Middle East and Central America.

Cold War warriors to peacemakers: Nixon and Brezhnev

Nixon and Brezhnev were unlikely peace makers. Nixon had built his career as an anti-communist in the US Senate and as Eisenhower's vice president. Brezhnev had been a senior figure in Moscow since the days of Stalin. Some have argued that their experiences helped them to understand what was at stake if tensions were allowed to increase once again.

SUMMARY

- By the late 1960s, tensions still remained between the superpowers, particularly over the issues of Vietnam and human rights.
- Détente was the result of a number of factors, including a desire to avoid a return to the brinkmanship of the first half of the decade.
- SALT I represented the most serious peace talks of the Cold War.

 **APPLY**

WRITE AN ACCOUNT

a   Create a spider diagram showing the reasons for détente.

b   What do you think was the most important reason for détente? Give reasons for your choices.

_____

_____

_____

_____

c   **EXAM QUESTION** Write an account of how international relations between the superpowers improved between the late 1960s and 1972.

EXAMINER TIP

Try to give two examples of improved relations between the superpowers.

Exam practice

GCSE sample answers

 REVIEW

On these exam practice pages, you will find a sample student answer for each of the exam questions for Paper 1: Section B: Conflict and Tension between East and West 1945–1972. What are the strengths and weaknesses of the answers? Read the following pages and think carefully about what the student has written, what the examiner has said about each answer, and how you might improve your own answers to Conflict and Tension exam questions.

Source analysis questions

▼ **SOURCE A** *An American cartoon by Roy Justus, published in the* Minneapolis Star *in 1947.*

EXAM QUESTION Study **Source A**. **Source A** supports the policies of the USA. How do you know? Explain your answer using **Source A** and your contextual knowledge.

4 marks

 REVISION SKILLS

You will always have two types of source questions in your Conflict and Tension exam. The first question (as here) deals with one source, the second question deals with two sources. Read page 8 for details on how to master your source analysis exam skills.

 EXAMINER TIP

The student uses specific evidence from the source and places it in a historical context; using their wider knowledge to explain what the symbolism means.

 EXAMINER TIP

More specific detail could be included about the USA's policies towards Western Europe.

Sample student answer

I know that the cartoon supports the policies of the USA because it shows the US Congress as a doctor racing towards Western Europe in order to help. The car is attempting to get to its destination before communism, represented by a vulture, delivers chaos. The doctor represents the American Government which is desperate to help Europe and prevent communism from developing there.

OVERALL COMMENT

This response would achieve a Level 2. The student explains the meaning of the details in the source and supports them with their own knowledge of the period.

OVER TO YOU

1 For this question it is important to balance the amount of detail that is required and the need to be concise.

  a Summarise the key features of the source in 4 bullet points.

  b Summarise the key features of USA policy towards Europe in 4 bullet points.

2 Reread the sample answer.

  a Highlight where the student has included specific details of the source.

  b Highlight where the student has shown specific contextual knowledge.

3 **a** Now have a go at writing your own answer. You should spend around 5 minutes on this type of question.

  b Review your answer. Did you…

    ☐ use specific evidence from the source?

    ☐ use your own knowledge and give at least one example of how the source supports USA policy?

    ☐ make sure your answer is focused on the question by using the same wording in your answer?

Go back to pages 20–21 to help refresh your knowledge of the policies of the USA directly after the Second World War.

▼ **SOURCE B** *A cartoon by E. H. Shepard. First published on 14 July 1948 in the British magazine* Punch.

THE BIRD WATCHER

▼ **SOURCE C** *Adapted from a US National Security Council memo, 6 October 1948:*

We are operating our planes into Berlin by right, and consequently any physical interference with that operation would be in violation of the Four-Powers Agreement. Such interferences would also be either a provocative or a hostile act on the part of the USSR. The National Security Council at its 16th Meeting on July 22, 1948 reiterated the determination of the United States to remain in Berlin in any event.

 EXAM QUESTION Study **Sources B** and **C**. How useful are **Sources B** and **C** to a historian studying the Berlin Airlift? Explain your answer using **Sources B** and **C** and your contextual knowledge.

12 marks

Sample student answer

Sources B and C are both useful to a historian studying the Berlin Airlift because they reflect different perspectives of the event. Source B is from the British satirical magazine 'Punch' and was published on 14 July 1948, just over two weeks after the start of the airlift. It shows birds carrying coal and food into Berlin while Stalin watches. The number of birds reflects the scale of the airlift, the like of which had never been seen before. Stalin is holding a gun but is not quite preparing to fire it. Instead, he is simply 'birdwatching'. The cartoon suggests that while Stalin may be very unhappy about this, he is unable to stop it and can only stand and watch it happen. While the actions of the Allies may be peaceful, war could very easily break out. The source reflects the concerns around the world about the consequences of the airlift, but in particular the unpredictability of Stalin.

Source C reflects the determination of the USA to remain in Berlin no matter the cost. As this is a government document that was not intended for publication it is likely to reflect the genuine thinking of the American government.

Both sources are useful because they show how close the airlift took the superpowers to war. Source C is useful because it shows that the airlift might have taken the superpowers to war demonstrating the determination of the American government to carry on regardless.

EXAMINER TIP

More contextual knowledge about the airlift would improve the answer here. For example, the answer could explain what the gun represents.

EXAMINER TIP

The answer makes specific reference to the provenance of the source and how this affects how useful it is.

OVERALL COMMENT

This is largely a Level 3 answer. It shows a good understanding of the sources in terms of content and provenance but there is room for more developed source analysis. In order to move into Level 4, it would need to use the sources together to make an inference from them both.

OVER TO YOU

1 How would you improve this answer?

  a Highlight in one colour the places where the answer explains the content of the sources.

  b Highlight in another colour where the answer explains the provenance of the sources and why this is important.

  c Highlight where the answer shows contextual knowledge of the Berlin Airlift.

  d Which areas require improvement?

2 Now have a go at writing your own answer. You should spend around 15 minutes on this type of question. Make sure you build on what you have discovered in question 1.

EXAMINER TIP

When analysing and evaluating a source it's a good idea to look at the provenance. This will help you decide how useful the source is – if it is one-sided or unreliable it may not be useful to a historian for the purpose stated in the question.

3 Review your answer. Did you:

☐ read the question carefully and make sure you addressed everything it asks you to do? For example, did you use both sources in your answer and explain them both?

☐ use details (a quote from a written source or a description of a visual source) as evidence to support your ideas?

☐ link each source to your own knowledge in order to evaluate their use to a historian studying the Berlin Airlift?

☐ use the information in the captions (provenance)? Go back to pages 24–25 to help refresh your knowledge of the Berlin Airlift.

The 'write an account' question

 EXAM QUESTION Write an account of how the Prague Spring led to increased tensions between the USSR and the West.

8 marks

Sample student answer

The Prague Spring and the Soviet response to it represented an important moment in relations between East and West. By the end of the 1960s, the difference in the standard of living either side of the Iron Curtain had become very clear. In Czechoslovakia in particular, there were growing calls for reform. In response, Moscow removed the unpopular leader of the country, Antonín Novotný, and replaced him with Alexander Dubček, whom they believed would calm the situation. Instead, Dubček began to introduce major reforms. Brezhnev, the Soviet leader, was in a difficult situation. Along with the other Warsaw Pact leaders, he was aware that allowing Czechoslovakia to continue on its path might encourage others to follow its example, but he was also aware the world was watching to see how much freedom there really was behind the Iron Curtain. His reluctance to act reflects the fact that he wanted to avoid making the crisis worse and risk the future of the communist bloc.

When the attempt to intimidate Dubček by holding military training exercises along the Czech border in June 1968, and the final threat of the Warsaw Letter, failed to solve the problem, Soviet tanks were sent into Czechoslovakia to remove Dubček and re-establish Soviet control. Moscow's aggression led to condemnation around the world. Communists in the West responded angrily but more significantly there was anger in non-Soviet communist countries, such as China and Yugoslavia. Relations between the USSR and China were severely damaged and communists elsewhere began to question how far the USSR was actually following the communist ideology.

 EXAMINER TIP

The answer tells the story of the Prague Spring, but there needs to be a more direct link to the question.

 EXAMINER TIP

The answer addresses the question here by explaining how the world responded to Soviet actions.

In the West, the USA condemned the USSRs actions and cancelled a meeting between Brezhnev and President Johnson. The UN attempted to pass a resolution condemning the violence. The Hungarian Uprising in 1956 had established that the USSR was allowed to do as it wished behind the Iron Curtain without Western interference, but the uprising damaged the USSR in the eyes of many people.

OVERALL COMMENT

This is a Level 3 answer. It shows contextual knowledge of the events of the Prague Spring and its consequences, but a greater focus on the question would improve the answer. It is important to remember that while the 'write an account' question should be narrative, it is also critical to have a developed explanation that answers the question. For every main point you make, check you have also included an effect or result that links directly to the focus of the question: in this question it is increased tensions.

OVER TO YOU

1   For a 'write an account' question you need to consider the events and their consequences.

   a Create a flow chart that shows the key events and consequences of the Prague Spring. Start with the calls for reform and finish with the reactions to the Soviet response around the world. Use pages 52–55 to help you.

2   Have a go at answering the question yourself. You should spend around 10 minutes on your answer. Use your flow chart to structure your answer; give details in chronological order and remember to explain what the effect or result of each event was.

3   Review your answer. Did you…

   ☐ explain at least two events that led to increased tensions during the Prague Spring?

   ☐ make sure your answer is focused on the question by using the same wording in your answer?

   ☐ make links between each event to show how tension grew?

EXAMINER TIP

Refer back to the question regularly as you write your answer, to make sure you are staying on track and answering exactly what the question is asking you.

The 'how far do you agree' question

 'The shooting down of the U2 spy plane was the main reason for an increase in tension between East and West between 1960 and 1962.'

How far do you agree with this statement? Explain your answer.

16 marks   SPaG 4 marks

EXAMINER TIP

Don't forget that you can pick up more marks here for showing the examiner that you can use spelling, punctuation and grammar correctly. It is worth factoring in some time to check your answer at the end. Make sure you write in paragraphs and that you use capital letters for proper nouns. Try to use historical terms – the glossary at the back of this book can help you become familiar with terms that could be useful in your exam.

Sample student answer

The shooting down of the U2 spy plane was a moment of high tension in the Cold War and damaged relations between the USSR and the USA. Although I agree that it was a major cause of the increased tension, there were a number of other reasons for the change in relations between 1960 and 1962. I would argue that the two leaders' responses to the crisis were in fact more important reasons for the increase in tension than the event itself.

The shooting down of the U2 spy plane and the subsequent trial of Francis Gary Powers came at a time of improving relations between the two sides. Eisenhower hoped to end his presidency by beginning a new age of co-operation. However, the existence of the spy plane proved that, far from trusting the USSR and co-operating, the USA was in fact spying on its rival. The wreckage and Powers himself were shown on Soviet television and there was no doubt what he had been doing in Soviet airspace. The existence of an American spy plane led to increased mistrust and therefore tension. Both sides were fully aware of the other's espionage programme, but the reactions of the leaders did lead to an increase in tension. Eisenhower's failure to admit that it was a spy plane further played into Khrushchev's desire to show that he was a strong leader who would stand up to the USA.

Another key reason for the increase in tension between 1960 and 1962 was the construction of the Berlin Wall in 1961. Berlin had remained an area of contention between the superpowers since its division in 1945. Khrushchev's decision to build the wall was officially to stop western spies from entering Soviet territory, but in reality it was a way of stopping East Germans from defecting to the West. It also stopped East Berliners from seeing the difference in the standard of living in the two halves of the city. The US government was angry about the wall and sent an official complaint. It was particularly annoyed that the wall had been built late on a Saturday night (USA time), delaying America's ability to respond. Later in the year Kennedy visited Berlin and made a speech in front of the wall. The president was sending a clear message to Khrushchev: the thaw between East and West that had been damaged by the U2 crisis had now been totally destroyed.

A final key factor in the increase in tension was the issue of Cuba. The rise of Castro greatly concerned the USA and its attempt to help overthrow him with the Bay of Pigs invasion angered the communist world. The real tension, however, developed over the issue of missiles. Khrushchev's decision to station nuclear weapons on Cuba and the reaction of Kennedy led to the highest point of tension in the Cold War. Neither leader was willing to back down and the superpowers came very close to nuclear war.

EXAMINER TIP

This introduction clearly addresses the question and sets out the argument that will be made.

EXAMINER TIP

Detailed contextual knowledge is demonstrated as the student explains the development of events. The student is also using phrases such as 'increased mistrust' and 'increase in tension', which link directly back to the question.

EXAMINER TIP

More specific detail about the Cuban Missile Crisis would have improved the answer here.

Overall, it is clear that the shooting down of the U2 spy plane was a moment of tension in the Cold War, but the main reason for the increase in tension between 1960 and 1962 was the Cuban Missile Crisis. While the shooting down of the U2 plane caused tensions, it was largely an opportunity for Khrushchev to build his own power, rather than a lasting serious crisis. The Soviet leader was keen to show that he was strong and would not be pushed around. The construction of the Berlin Wall was also a clear moment of tension but the USA's measured response meant that things did not escalate. During the Cuban Missile Crisis, however, tensions were so high that there were moments when events were way beyond the control of the two leaders.

EXAMINER TIP

The conclusion makes direct comparisons between the three events and comes to a clear judgement about which was the biggest cause of tension.

OVERALL COMMENT

This is a Level 3 answer. The response has a clear structure that addresses the question and comes to a judgement. It considers several causes of tension during the period and comes to a developed conclusion. More detail about the Cuban Missile Crisis and how it led to tension would have added more depth to the answer.

OVER TO YOU

1 What are the strengths of this answer? Read it through and highlight the positive elements.

2 What could be improved? Try to make at least two additions that would improve its quality.

3 Have a go at writing your own answer. You should spend around 20 minutes on your answer. Once you have written it, review your answer. Did you:

- [ ] include specific historical detail?
- [ ] explain more than one reason for the increase in tension?
- [ ] link back to the question regularly to keep your answer focused on the question?
- [ ] use accurate spelling, punctuation and grammar?
- [ ] come to a clear judgement that fully addresses the question?

Go back to pages 40 and 41 to help refresh your knowledge of the tensions between East and West in 1960.

EXAMINER TIP

Be careful in the exam: read the questions carefully and make sure that you always answer what is asked, rather than a question you've revised.

The answers provided here are examples, based on the information provided in the Recap sections of this Revision Guide. There may be other factors that are relevant to each question, and you should draw on as much of your own knowledge as possible to give detailed and precise answers. There are also many ways of answering exam questions (for example, of structuring an essay). However, these exemplar answers should provide a good starting point.

Chapter 1 Page 13

HOW FAR DO YOU AGREE?

a Poster should include key differences shown in table, e.g. free market vs controlled economy; multi-party vs one party; and private business vs state ownership.

b Set of flashcards including areas of distrust such as: ideological differences; propaganda; First World War; Russian Civil War; Stalin's regime; Nazi–Soviet Pact. Cards in justified order of importance. Example of justification could be: 'The Russian Civil War demonstrated that the West could never work with the East because it opposed communism from the beginning.'

c Answer is likely to include:

Agree: ideological differences were important because communism and capitalism were totally opposed. Communism's aim was to overthrow capitalism and the West therefore saw it as a threat.

Disagree: other factors were more important. Ideological differences were theoretical, whereas Soviet withdrawal from the First World War and the Western involvement in the Russian Civil War were clear evidence that the sides could not trust each other.

Page 15

HOW FAR DO YOU AGREE?

a Example could include:

Stalin/FDR: Desire to rebuild Europe and work together.

Churchill/FDR: Europe should be capitalist; creation of World Bank.

Churchill/Stalin: Percentages agreement.

All three: Rebuild Europe; United Nations.

b Answer could suggest: They had the same aims in that there was a desire to work together and to rebuild Europe. They did not have the same aims in that they disagreed about the idea of a sphere of influence and whether Europe should be rebuilt under a capitalist or a communist system.

c Answer could argue: Stalin because he kept the idea of a sphere of influence on the table; Roosevelt and Churchill because of the UN and the Declaration of Liberated Europe, all three because they achieved some aspect of what they wanted; or no one because nothing was firmly decided.

d Answer is likely to include:

Agree: Stalin wanted to avoid future conflict with the Western allies and the agreements allowed this; the division of Germany gave Stalin the buffer zone he desired and left Germany weakened; the Red Army remained in Eastern Europe despite the plan for free elections.

Disagree: the division of Berlin gave the Western allies a foothold in Eastern Europe; Eastern European countries were to be given free elections – this put the idea of a buffer zone at risk.

Page 17

SOURCE ANALYSIS

a Answer might include: It suggests that Stalin was relaxed whereas Truman was not; Truman was well prepared and fixed in his thinking and Stalin was also unwilling to compromise.

b An example answer could be: The source shows Truman suggesting that they 'can work together in mutual trust and confidence' and sharing his '12 points' with Stalin and Attlee. Stalin and Attlee appear to be considering Truman's ideas. Truman, however, is holding an atomic bomb, marked 'private'.

c It is making the point that while Truman talked of peace and co-operation, he was in fact keeping the development of the atomic bomb secret from his allies.

d Answer is likely to include:

- Sources A and B are useful because they give a sense of the relationship between the leaders.

- Although they are both from 1945, Source A is from before, and Source B is from after, the dropping of the atomic bombs on Japan.

- Source A shows that the tensions were already building at Potsdam because neither side was willing to compromise.

- Source B suggests that Truman's secrecy over the bomb was a major cause of tension.

WRITE AN ACCOUNT

a The key areas of disagreement were: The future of Eastern Europe (self-determination or Soviet influence); whether Germany should pay reparations.

b The problems that remained were: The future of Eastern Europe (the Red Army occupied the majority of it); tensions over the atomic bomb; it became very difficult for non-communists to gain power in the countries occupied by the Red Army.

c Answer is likely to include: It led to an increase in tension because it established a long-term division of Germany, without a plan for how to resolve the issue; Truman did not tell Stalin about the atomic bomb; the fact that the Red Army already occupied Eastern Europe meant that Stalin had a significant advantage in the negotiations.

Chapter 2 Page 19

SOURCE ANALYSIS

a The source shows the Iron Curtain dividing Europe in two, by order of 'Joe' (Stalin). Eastern Europe is being rebuilt behind the curtain while Western Europe remains empty. Churchill is trying to see what is happening behind the curtain.

b Answer might include:

- It shows a clear physical division between East and West in the form of the giant curtain.

- The 'No admittance' sign shows that separation is total.

- 'By order of Joe' shows that it was a deliberate decision made by Stalin.
- The signpost pointing directly to the wall suggests that dialogue with Russia is blocked.
- The evidence of destroyed buildings in the top left-hand corner contrasts with the busy industry on the other side of the Iron Curtain and suggests criticism of Soviet unwillingness to help with the rebuilding of Europe as a whole.
- What is happening in the USSR is hidden from the prying eyes of the West. The USSR has something to hide.
- Russia is building up its economic/military strength.
- Guards on the wall suggest military enforcement.
- The reaction of people in the West is a mixture of disbelief and terror.

WRITE AN ACCOUNT

a Fact sheet should include key elements of the Long Telegram (written by G. Kennan; sent in 1946; said that the USSR could not be trusted and wanted to control Europe) and the Iron Curtain Speech (given by Churchill in 1946; described the division of Europe and Soviet aims).

b Answer might include:
- Until August 1945, the USSR and the Western Allies were still working together against Nazi Germany and Japan.
- At the Potsdam Conference, they still talked about co-operation.
- The Long Telegram and Iron Curtain speech led to mistrust and division.
- However, the seeds of mistrust were already present in 1945 due to the atomic bomb and Soviet influence in Eastern Europe.

Page 21
SOURCE ANALYSIS

a You should produce your own mind-map including key aims and details of the Truman Doctrine and the Marshall Plan.

b Source A shows a man, who represents Europe, climbing up a cliff using a rope. The rope is labelled 'the Marshall Plan'.

He is climbing away from communism, which is represented by the red and the Russian-style buildings at the bottom of the cliff.

c Source A suggests that the Marshall Plan helped Europe escape communism and that, without it, Europe would have fallen under Soviet influence.

d Source B describes Stalin's view of the Marshall Plan. He saw it as an attempt by the USA to infiltrate and influence European countries.

e Source B sees the Marshall Plan differently to Source A. It sees it as the USA using money to gain influence over Europe, rather than providing an escape. Unlike Source A, which is American, this source is from an interview with a former Soviet minister.

f Answers might include:

Source A is useful because it shows one of the key aims of Marshall Aid: to stop the whole of Europe falling to communism. It is an American cartoon, published in 1947; and reflects the US view of the Marshall Plan and its purpose.

Source B is useful because it shows the Soviet view of the Marshall Plan by someone close to Stalin who would know and understand what Stalin thought about it. The Soviets believed it was an attempt by the US to increase its control and influence over Europe.

Page 23
HOW FAR DO YOU AGREE?

a You should produce your own spider diagram, which needs to include Cominform and Comecon.

b Answer might include: It led to further division because it united the East in the same way as the Marshall Plan united the West; it increased tension and mistrust between the sides; it increased Stalin's grip on Eastern Europe.

c Answer might include:

The USA was most responsible because the Truman Doctrine showed that it was unwilling to work with the USSR, and, although the Marshall Plan was

open to all countries, it was always clear that the USSR would not allow countries in the East to accept it.

The USSR was most responsible because of Stalin's decision not to allow Eastern European countries to accept Marshall Aid, and the creation of Cominform and Comecon created two distinct and separate halves of Europe.

d Answer is likely to include:

Agree: The Marshall Plan only rebuilt Western Europe, which led to division and rivalry; it was seen as American interference; the Truman Doctrine made it clear that it had a political motive.

Disagree: Cominform helped to tighten Stalin's grip on Eastern Europe; Comecon was a deliberate attempt to unite Eastern Europe, which led to division and rivalry.

SOURCE ANALYSIS

a Source A shows an argument between Stalin and Tito, the leader of Yugoslavia. The people in the street are ordinary Yugoslavians who are fearful of the consequences of the argument.

b The source is depicting the disagreement between Stalin and Tito in 1948 over Tito's decision to accept Marshall Aid.

c Answer might include: Stalin and Tito are shown as neighbours arguing but Stalin is threatening Tito by waving his fist; the cartoon was created in 1948, when their disagreement took place. Stalin looks aggressive and the people below, who are ordinary Yugoslavians, look worried.

Page 25
WRITE AN ACCOUNT

a Timeline is likely to include: March 1948 – Unification of Western sector; April 1948 – Mini blockade; 24 June 1948 – beginning of full blockade; 26 June 1948 – Airlift begins; 15 April 1949 – 'Easter Parade'; 12 May 1949 – Blockade ends; 23 May 1949 – Creation of the FDR; October 1949 – Creation of the GDR.

b Answer might include:
  - Relations between East and West were relatively strong in 1945 when the division of Berlin/Germany was agreed.
  - Tensions increased as Stalin tried to gain more control over East Germany.
  - Tensions increased when the Western Allies unified their sectors.
  - The blockade increased tensions drastically.
  - During the Berlin Airlift, tensions were the worst they had ever been.

SOURCE ANALYSIS

a Answer might include:
  - The Russian bear is enclosing the whole of Berlin within its arms, including the Western sector.
  - The bear's claws are about to close the final access point. The claws are red, the colour of communism.
  - The red on the claws could also be blood. The USSR is being a predator. Berlin is its prey.

Chapter 3 Page 27
SOURCE ANALYSIS

a The source suggests that Stalin's support for Mao's China was not actually that helpful. By providing a 'shovel', all he is doing is causing the death of many Chinese soldiers.

b Answer is likely to include: The source is critical of the USSR because it shows Stalin looking on and pretending to help Mao when, in fact, Mao and China are doing all of the hard work and sacrificing the men in order to support Stalin and the USSR.

HOW FAR DO YOU AGREE?

a You should produce your own mind-map showing key information about the communist revolution in China and how the West and the USSR responded. You might include how Mao took control, Western concerns over the spread of communism into Asia and their refusal to recognise the new government, and the Soviet support for the People's Republic of China.

b An example answer might include: It was important because it showed that communism was still popular and that the policy of containment was not working. It gave Stalin confidence and made the USA concerned about the rest of Asia. As a result, they increased military spending.

c Answer is likely to include:

Agree: the communist takeover in China created a second, large and powerful communist country; it reinforced the idea of the Domino Theory; it created a communist power in Asia that was not directly controlled by the USSR.

Disagree: there were other reasons for tension including the U2 crisis; tensions over Berlin, including the wall and Kennedy's visit; Cuba.

Page 29
WRITE AN ACCOUNT

a You should produce your own storyboard, including:
  - The division of Korea and its two leaders
  - Kim asking Stalin for weapons
  - The invasion by North Korea
  - The UN invasion
  - Chinese involvement
  - The ceasefire.

b Answer might include:
  - Description of events in Korea, including the causes, events and consequences of the war.
  - The war in a wider context, e.g. focus of Cold War moves to Asia; proxy war; increased tensions; role of China.

Page 31
SOURCE ANALYSIS

a It suggests that Vietnam was important because of the Domino Theory. If Vietnam fell to communism, its neighbours would follow.

b It is based on comments by President Eisenhower. As he was the one making decisions, this makes it useful for understanding American thinking on Vietnam.

c It suggests that the USA wants to stop another Asian country falling to communism. The USA, represented by Uncle Sam, is sailing directly towards an iceberg. The iceberg is covered in the headstones of the countries that have already fallen to communism. Uncle Sam is totally unaware of the danger.

d Answer might include:

Source A is useful because it describes the Domino Theory and comes directly from the US president, Dwight D. Eisenhower.

Source B is useful because it shows that the USA is trying to stop countries falling to communism but that it is not succeeding. The cartoon is from 1960, by which time a number of Asian countries has become communist and US advisors were in Vietnam trying to prevent that country falling to communism.

WRITE AN ACCOUNT

a Spiral might include: French withdrawal; division of Vietnam; establishment of Vietcong; Ho Chi Minh trail; assassination of Diem.

b Answer must be explained, e.g. the point at which it became inevitable was the establishment of the Vietcong because it was clear at that point that the South Vietnamese government was at serious risk of collapsing.

c Answer might include: the USA became increasingly involved in the Vietnam War because of its belief in the Domino Theory. The fall of China to communism meant that the USA feared Vietnam would be next. After the French withdrawal, North Vietnam became communist and the USA sent advisors to South Vietnam. As the communists became more popular, the USA became increasingly involved in the conflict.

Chapter 4 Page 33
SOURCE ANALYSIS

a An example answer could be: The source shows the countries of NATO playing cards with Stalin. They are waiting to see what Stalin's next move will be.

b An example answer could be: The source is suggesting that while the formation of NATO gives the West strength against Stalin, they are still waiting for his next move.

c Answer might include: It is useful because it shows that NATO united the West but that Stalin remained an unpredictable figure. Harry Truman is sitting at the front of the group, reflecting the fact that the USA provided most of the money and fire power in NATO.

d   Answer might include: Source A shows NATO playing cards with Stalin across Europe, NATO's theatre of action. The West have created NATO and are waiting to see how Stalin and the USSR react; the West is in control.

WRITE AN ACCOUNT

a   You should produce your own revision cards. Facts might include: Warsaw Pact – nuclear weapons held by the USSR; NATO – nuclear weapons held by USA, Britain and France.

b   Reasons might include:

NATO: Growing strength of the USSR, including the nuclear bomb; tensions and risk of war presented by the Berlin Blockade; the desire to contain communism.

Warsaw Pact: the formation of NATO; the admittance of West Germany to NATO; the Korean War (increased risk of direct armed conflict); a desire by the USSR to control Eastern Europe more firmly, especially following Stalin's death.

c   Answer might include: It led to increased tension because it cemented the idea of the two united sides facing each other; it increased US involvement and influence in Western Europe and strengthened Soviet control in Eastern Europe; the idea that attack on one NATO member would be seen as an attack on all made war more likely.

Page 35

WRITE AN ACCOUNT

a/b   Graph will include all of the events shown on the timeline. They should be placed in the appropriate area, based on whether they were good for the USSR or for the USA.

c   Answer might point out:

*   The USSR was in the lead for much of the race and achieved many firsts, including the first satellite, the first animal and the first man in space.

*   The USA victory in getting a man to the moon suggested that, by the end of the 1960s, the USA was ahead.
*   The joint mission suggests co-operation and the end of the space race.

d   Answer might include: The space race shows the rivalry between the two sides throughout the 1950s, 1960s and the first half of the 1970s; the joint mission in 1975 reflected the improved relations between the two superpowers at the time.

SOURCE ANALYSIS

a   Source A suggests that the USA, or at least Vice President Johnson, recognised that space exploration would show the USA was the world's leader.

b   Source A was written by Vice President Johnson on 28 April 1961. This was seven days before Kennedy's promise to land a man on the moon by the end of the decade. At this point the USA was lagging behind the USSR in its achievements in space.

c   Source B shows that the USSR saw success in the space race as an important source of propaganda. The cartoon shows Gagarin, having returned from space, meeting with Khrushchev. While the Soviet leader is pleased with the achievement, he is suggesting that it would have been better if Gagarin had seen the world as red (the colour of communism) rather than blue. The cartoon is suggesting that the Soviets saw the space race as a way to appear superior to the USA and the rest of the world.

d   Answer might include:

Source A is useful because it shows the thoughts of a senior member of the American government. It is an internal memo to the President so was not created to be seen by the wider public; it is therefore likely to reflect actual government thinking. The fact that it is from just a few days before Kennedy's famous 'moon shot' speech shows that the USA government saw success in the space race as very important.

Source B is useful because it is an Australian cartoon and therefore not produced by either of the superpowers. It is important to note, however, that Australia was an ally of the USA in the Cold War. It suggests that the USSR saw the space race as a propaganda tool in order to increase its global influence. The fact that Khrushchev wants Gagarin to wear red-tinted glasses suggests that propaganda is more important than scientific discovery or achievement.

Page 37

HOW FAR DO YOU AGREE?

a   You should produce your own mind-map. It might include causes, key events, key developments and consequences.

b   Answer might include:

Agree: the arms race began after the Americans failed to reveal their nuclear weapons to the Soviets before using them to end the Second World War; neither side trusted the motives of the other, particularly over tension points like Berlin, Korea and Cuba.

Disagree: each side saw the other as a genuine threat and the proxy wars demonstrated that this was justified; the existence of powerful nuclear arsenals was more about status than war; MAD meant that simply by owning the weapons, the two sides were able to protect themselves from attack.

WRITE AN ACCOUNT

a/b   You should produce your own colour-coded timeline and include all of the categories suggested in the question, as well as any others you feel are significant.

Chapter 5 Page 39

WRITE AN ACCOUNT

a   You should produce your own storyboard. It should include the situation before the uprising, the uprising itself and the USSR's response.

b   Answer might include: The call for reforms and the Soviet response was widely seen as brutal and disproportionate: this led to anger in the West. The majority of the UN wanted to condemn the USSR's actions but the USSR vetoed it. The USA did not become involved because events took place behind the Iron Curtain.

HOW FAR DO YOU AGREE?

a Answer might include:

Khrushchev was concerned that the reforms had gone too far and the USSR would lose a satellite state. He believed that events in Hungary could inspire others and weaken the Eastern Bloc, which could in turn lead to a weakened USSR and the loss of the Cold War.

b Answer is likely to include:

Agree: the West condemned the brutality of the Soviet response. It damaged the USSR's reputation and therefore raised tensions. It also contradicted Khrushchev's promise of a different approach and de-Stalinisation.

Disagree: the West was not concerned about events behind the Iron Curtain and did not want them to disrupt improving relations. The international community was also more concerned by other events, such as the Suez Crisis.

Page 41
SOURCE ANALYSIS

a The source is referring to the shooting down of the U2 spy plane and the subsequent failure of the Paris Peace Summit. The evidence is that the plane, which is labelled 'U2', has collided with a dove, the symbol of peace. Khrushchev and the Americans are standing on the sides of the mountain, just short of the top – the summit.

b Answer might include:

We know because it shows a U2 plane crashing into a dove, which is the symbol of peace. Khrushchev and the Americans have stopped climbing towards the summit of the mountain because of the crash.

HOW FAR DO YOU AGREE?

a You should produce your own flow chart, including the events listed in the question and any others you feel are significant.

b Answer might include:

Agree: some argue that Khrushchev wanted the summit to fail because he believed that the USSR had the upper hand in the Cold War and he wanted to show his rivals in Moscow that he was tough. The Soviet response to the U2 crisis, as well as events in Hungary, showed aggression and damaged the improving relations between East and West.

Disagree: a key reason for the summit's failure was the U2 spy plane and the Americans refusal to admit the truth. This showed the USA to be untrustworthy and severely damaged relations.

Chapter 6 Page 43
SOURCE ANALYSIS

a Source A suggests that the wall was built:

- in order to prevent people defecting from East to West (particularly engineers) – 'Many educated people, scientists and engineers, have fled the GDR', 'to stop this loss of key people'
- as a means of pressure in negotiations with the West – 'the current tensions...present a good opportunity', 'we can use it as a bargaining tool'

It also says that they could claim it was built because of the threat of war – 'we can explain it because we feel threatened with war and want to keep out spies.'

b Source B suggests that the wall was built to stop people leaving East Berlin: the arms and bodies of people flung over the wall from the east side imply many are attempting to leave. It agrees with Source A that the reason for building the wall was to prevent the loss of skilled workers and professionals from East Germany. However, Source A suggests that Khrushchev had another reason for building the wall – he wanted to use it as a bargaining chip in negotiations.

c Answer might include:

Source A is useful because it explains two of the main reasons for the wall being built. There was a serious

problem with skilled and educated people leaving East Berlin and Khrushchev was in talks with Kennedy at the time and wanted to show strength. It is also useful because it is from a private meeting between two very senior figures and certainly not intended to be read by the public.

Source B is useful because it reflects the US view of why the wall was built.

Page 45
HOW FAR DO YOU AGREE?

a It led to tensions because: it created a visual divide in Europe; it split families; it limited Western knowledge of events behind the Iron Curtain; it caused a serious moment of tension in October 1961 when there was a standoff on the border.

b It did not lead to increased tension because: it did not encroach on Western Berlin; Kennedy did not want a war; it largely settled the situation in Berlin.

c Answer might include:

Agree: it cemented the divide in Europe; it split families; it limited Western knowledge of events behind the Iron Curtain and therefore led to further distrust; it caused a serious moment of tension in October 1961 when there was a standoff on the border.

Disagree: it did not encroach on West Berlin, and was therefore behind the Iron Curtain; Kennedy did not want a war and so accepted it; it largely settled the situation in Berlin and the Cold War focus moved elsewhere.

Chapter 7 Page 47
SOURCE ANALYSIS

a Source A shows Castro pushing pins into voodoo dolls while Khrushchev and Mao watch. (Voodoo – black magic – dolls are made to represent a certain person; by hurting the dolls, that person is hurt or influenced in real life.) The dolls are labelled with the names of South American countries. The pins he is using are in the shape of the hammer and sickle (the symbols of communism). The source is suggesting that Castro's victory will lead to communism elsewhere.

b Answer might include: The source is critical because it shows Castro is a threat because he is causing communism to spread to South America; Mao and Khrushchev have influence over him.

HOW FAR DO YOU AGREE?

a You should produce your own timeline. It might include: the Batista government; Castro's revolution; the Bay of Pigs; increasingly close relationship between Castro and the USSR.

b Answer might include:

Agree: American businesses were part of the corruption that led to Castro's rise; Eisenhower refused to meet with Castro; the US placed an embargo on Cuba; it launched the Bay of Pigs invasion to try to remove Castro from power.

Disagree: Castro seized American businesses and land and aligned himself with the Soviet Union; the USSR gave aid to the Cuban government, which angered the USA.

Page 49
SOURCE ANALYSIS

a Source A shows Kennedy and Khrushchev arm-wrestling. They are each sitting on a nuclear weapon, with the finger of their other hand hovering over a launch button connected to the weapons.

b The source is saying that the crisis is a battle of strength between the two leaders but that there is an underlying threat of nuclear war.

c Source B outlines what could have gone wrong had Kennedy's strategy not worked. It asks what the consequences would have been had the USSR responded in a different way. It is critical of President Kennedy, suggesting that he was reckless.

d Answer might include:

Source A is useful because it reflects the reality of the Cuban Missile Crisis by showing that while Kennedy and

Khrushchev argued (or 'arm wrestled'), nuclear weapons were present and could easily come into play. Their fingers are hovering over nuclear launch buttons. It is a British cartoon published on 29 October 1962, just after the crisis.

Source B is useful because it considers the implications had the USSR called the Americans' bluff. It is critical of Kennedy's actions and suggests that he was reckless. The fact that the source was published after Kennedy's assassination, a year after the crisis, allows for some hindsight but also recognises that Kennedy's murder may have affected people's assessment of his achievements and caused them to be seen in a more positive light.

HOW FAR DO YOU AGREE?

a You should produce your own timeline. It should include the key developments, beginning with the arrival of Soviet missiles on Cuba and ending with their removal.

b List might include:

the arrival of missiles in Cuba, the blockade, Soviet ships sailing towards the blockade, the oil tanker entering the quarantine area, the US troops in Florida, the submarine incident, the shooting down of the US plane, the US plane in Soviet airspace.

Examples of importance could be: the US troops in Florida were important because it showed the USA was preparing for an invasion. The shooting down of the US plane was important because it could have triggered a war.

c Answer might include:

Agree: Kennedy ordered the blockade and assembled troops, knowing that it would cause tension.

Disagree: Khrushchev placed missiles in Cuba and threatened to break the blockade; events beyond the control of the leaders could have led to nuclear war (submarine and plane incidents).

Page 51
SOURCE ANALYSIS

a Source A suggests that Kennedy and Khrushchev are keen to avoid a repeat

of the Cuban Missile Crisis by 'getting a lock' for the monster nuclear weapons. It also suggests they both want to work together to achieve this.

b Source B suggests that Kennedy wanted the Cuban Missile Crisis to represent a change in relations between East and West around the world.

c Answer might include:

Source A is useful because it shows that both Kennedy and Khrushchev were keen to avoid the risks of brinkmanship again. Their struggle to close the box suggests that it will not be easy. The cartoon is from the widely read American newspaper the *Washington Post*. It is likely to represent a widely held view.

Source B is useful because it shows what Kennedy hoped the crisis would lead to – a decrease in tensions and the end of the arms race. However, it is important to note that it is an official statement, and therefore represents what the government or President wanted the citizens to believe was the official policy.

Chapter 8 Page 53
SOURCE ANALYSIS

a The cartoon shows Dubček meeting Brezhnev and other Warsaw Pact leaders. The leaders are pretending they want to discuss the situation, but in reality they are ready to use violence. Soviet soldiers are badly disguised as secretaries and the tanks are labelled as typewriters.

b Answer might include: We know because the source shows the Warsaw Pact leaders pretending to come in peace and discuss the crisis, while preparing for an invasion. This is shown through the disguised soldiers and tanks.

Page 55
WRITE AN ACCOUNT

a You should produce your own mind-map. Branches should include: Czechoslovakia before the Prague Spring; Dubček's reforms; the Warsaw Pact's military exercises; the Warsaw Letter; the Soviet invasion.

b Answer might include: the reforms of Dubček and how this challenged the Soviet system that has existed before the response of the Warsaw Pact, including the decision to conduct military exercises near the border and the Warsaw Letter, and their concern that allowing the reforms to continue could cause unrest in their own countries.

HOW FAR DO YOU AGREE?

a Consequences included: the Soviet invasion of Czechoslovakial; criticism of the USSR by communists abroad, including China; the establishment of the Brezhnev Doctrine; Western condemnation but no action.

b The most important consequence needs to be explained, e.g. the criticism of the Soviet response by China opened the possibility of improved relations between the USA and China. This was a key factor in Détente.

c Answer is likely to include:

Agree: Relations with China were damaged; there were protests in other Eastern European capitals, including a very minor protest in Moscow; communist parties in the West became less popular because the USSR was now seen as an empire forcing its control on weaker countries and oppressing people.

Disagree: The USSR remained in control in Czechoslovakia and had shown that it could not be challenged; the West did not become involved in the conflict because it took place behind the Iron Curtain and so Moscow's power was not challenged.

Chapter 9 Page 57

WRITE AN ACCOUNT

a You should produce your own spider diagram. Branches could include: the China-Soviet split; the nuclear issue, the economic issue, the lessons of conflict.

b Answer should give a reason for the chosen decision, e.g. the nuclear issue because the Cuban Missile Crisis showed that neither side wanted to risk nuclear war.

c Answer might include: the China-Soviet split and the improved relations between the USA and the People's Republic of China; the nuclear issue and the desire to avoid brinkmanship; the USA's experience in Vietnam and desire to avoid a repeat; the cost of the Cold War, particularly for the USSR, which was overspending in order to keep up.

boycotting refusing to buy goods or services from someone for political reasons

de-Stalinisation the period after Stalin's death in which Khrushchev tried to make changes to the USSR

détente improving relations between the USSR and the USA during the 1970s

dollar imperialism the idea that the USA spreads its influence and power around the world using money

Domino Theory the theory followed in the USA from Eisenhower onwards that communism would make countries fall like dominoes; when one country becomes communist, its neighbours would soon fall too

House Un-American Activities Committee (HUAC) the committee in the US House of Representatives that pursued and investigated those suspected of being involved in 'Un-American' (communist) activity

ideology a guiding political belief, e.g. communism

International Monetary Fund (IMF) an organisation that oversees the world's economies

Kremlin the headquarters of the Soviet government in Moscow during the Cold War; previously the palace of the tsar, now the residence of the Russian president

Mutually Assured Destruction (MAD) the idea that the full-scale use of nuclear weapons by opposing sides will cause the complete destruction of all involved

New Look the defence policy followed by US President Eisenhower

proxy war an indirect war between the superpowers where the USA or USSR fund the other enemy; examples include Korea, Vietnam and Angola

Red Scare the widespread fear of communism; it usually refers to the 1920s in the USA but can also refer to other points in the Cold War such as during the McCarthy era of the 1950s

Secretary of State the US chief diplomat – the equivalent of the UK's Foreign Secretary

self-determination the right for people to choose how their country should be governed

sphere of influence the idea that the USSR and the USA would have countries or regions that were under their 'influence' after the Second World War; for Stalin, this was a way of guaranteeing security

trade union an organisation of workers, usually in a particular industry, that protects their interests, negotiates pay rates and improves working conditions

Treaty of Friendship an agreement made between the USSR and China in 1950

unilateral disarmament the policy of giving up nuclear weapons without an agreement from other countries to do the same

United Nations an international organisation that aims to stop conflict and encourage cooperation between countries; it was formed after the Second World War

veto the right to overrule a decision

Vietcong the communist guerrilla fighters in Vietnam

Viet Minh Vietnamese communists, supporters of Ho Chi Minh

World Bank an international organisation that provides loans to help countries to develop